AMISH INSPIRATIONS

QUILT
PATTERNS • DESIGNS • IDEAS

BY SUZY LAWSON

• **FULL SIZE PATTERNS AND TEMPLATES FOR 46 COMPLETE QUILTS** •
SCALE DRAWINGS OF FINISHED QUILTS
WITH BORDER MEASUREMENTS
AND QUILT DIMENSIONS

• **38 FULL SIZE QUILTING MOTIFS** •
A WIDE VARIETY WITH TEMPLATES
AND INSTRUCTIONS FOR DESIGNING MORE OF YOUR OWN

• **12 ADDITIONAL BORDER VARIATIONS TO AID IN DESIGNING** •

• **HELPS AND HOW-TO'S ON COLOR, FABRIC AND DESIGN** •

PUBLISHED BY
AMITY PUBLICATIONS
78688 SEARS ROAD
COTTAGE GROVE, OREGON 97424-9470

CREDITS

PUBLISHED BY: AMITY PUBLICATIONS
              78688 SEARS ROAD
              COTTAGE GROVE, OREGON 97424-9470

PRINTED IN THE UNITED STATES OF AMERICA.

LIBRARY OF CONGRESS CATALOG CARD NUMBER: 82-72353

ISBN 0-943814-00-6

COVER PHOTOGRAPHY BY: PAT BURT CREATIVE PHOTOGRAPHY
                      1412 SE STARK
                      PORTLAND, OREGON 97214

PHOTOGRAPHED AT THE OXBARN MUSEUM IN AURORA, OREGON.
COURTESY OF THE AURORA HISTORICAL SOCIETY.

FABRIC IN PHOTOGRAPHS COURTESY OF: THE PATCHWORK PEDDLER QUILT SHOP
                                   3614 N.E. BROADWAY
                                   PORTLAND, OREGON

ALL DRAWINGS AND ILLUSTRATIONS ARE BY THE AUTHOR.
ALL QUILTS AND ITEMS PHOTOGRAPHED WERE MADE BY THE AUTHOR.
"WINDMILL BLADES" QUILT ON FRONT COVER WAS QUILTED BY
SHIRLEY MILLER, COTTAGE GROVE, OREGON.

PRINTED BY: EUGENE PRINT
            20 EAST 13TH
            EUGENE, OREGON 97401

ACKNOWLEDGEMENTS

SPECIAL LOVE AND GRATITUDE TO MY HUSBAND AND PARTNER DAVID AND CHILDREN DOVE, TIA AND SETH WHO CONTINUALLY MAKE AVAILABLE TO ME THEIR UNCONDITIONAL LOVE AND SUPPORT AND SOME SPACE WHEN I NEED IT.

MUCH LOVE AND APPRECIATION TO MY GOOD FRIEND AND NEIGHBOR DOROTHY BOND AND MY FRIENDS AND ASSOCIATES SUZI BLUCHER, BEV SOASEY, ROXY BURGARD AND DIANE CHRISTENSEN WHO PROVIDE ME WITH ASSISTANCE, ENCOURAGEMENT AND INSPIRATION. TO ALL MY OTHER QUILTING FRIENDS AND TO MY FRIEND COLLEEN ALLEN, FOR BEING SO SUPPORTIVE, I GIVE THANKS.

THANK YOU TO ALL OF MY STUDENTS WHOSE ENTHUSIASM AND ZEAL HAVE CONTRIBUTED GREATLY TO MY LIFE AND MY QUILTMAKING.

"The Lord is my strength and my song; he has become my salvation. He is my God, and I will praise him, my father's God, and I will exalt him."
                    Exodus 15:2

KEY TO COVER PHOTOGRAPHS

FRONT COVER

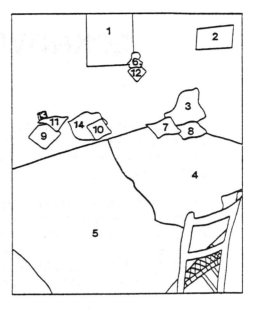

1. *AMISH BASKET SAMPLER
2. INTERLOCKING SQUARES
3. STARBURST AND STRIPES
4. DOUBLE IRISH CHAIN
5. WINDMILL BLADES
6. *AMISH DOLL
7-12. *CENTER DIAMOND AND
       BARS VARIATIONS
13. *MINEATURE CENTER DIAMOND
    PIN CUSHION
14. *DOLL QUILT

BACK COVER

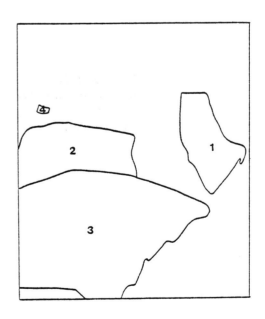

1. BOW TIE
2. ROMAN STRIPES
3. STAR WITHIN A STAR
4. *BASKET PIN CUSHION

* - INDICATES PATTERNS AVAILABLE FROM THE PUBLISHER.
    SEND S.A.S.E. FOR ORDERING INFORMATION.

    PATTERNS FOR THE OTHER QUILTS PHOTOGRAPHED ARE IN
    THIS BOOK. SEE TABLE OF CONTENTS.

TABLE OF CONTENTS

INTRODUCTION

THIS IS NOT AN HISTORICAL DOCUMENTATION. THERE ARE MANY FINE BOOKS AND ARTICLES AVAILABLE FOR THOSE WANTING TO STUDY THE AMISH AND THEIR CULTURE IN DETAIL. THIS IS A BOOK OF PATTERNS, DESIGNS AND IDEAS BASED ON THE AMISH CONCEPTS AND UNWRITTEN RULES GOVERNING QUILTMAKING, AS I SEE THEM, FROM A PERIOD CONSISTING OF ABOUT 60 YEARS. (THE LATE 1800'S TO THE EARLY 1930'S)

IT IS NOT MY INTENTION TO EXPLOIT THESE MOST PRIVATE PEOPLE AND THEIR QUILTS, BUT RATHER TO INTERPRET AND PRESERVE THEIR DESIGNS FOR QUILTMAKERS WHO, LIKE MYSELF, ADMIRE THEM TO THE POINT OF WANTING TO MAKE. ONE.

THE FIRST AMISH QUILT I SAW CONTRADICTED MY ASSUMPTION THAT ALL AMISH QUILTS WOULD BE DARK IN COLOR AND VISUALLY VERY PLAIN. AS I SEARCHED FURTHER I DISCOVERED QUILTS WITH COLORS THAT HAD AN ELECTRICAL EFFECT AND DESIGNS THAT WERE VERY CONTEMPORARY IN THEIR APPEAL. FOR ME, IT WAS THE BEGINNING OF A NEW ADVENTURE IN QUILTMAKING. I KNEW I HAD TO OWN SOME OF THESE SPECTACULAR QUILTS AND, AS A QUILTMAKER, THE MOST PRACTICAL AND LOGICAL APPROACH WAS TO MAKE THEM. AS I BEGAN EXPLORING THE AMISH QUILT WORLD IN SEARCH OF COLOR AND DESIGN I WAS AMAZED AT THE DIVERSITY OF PATTERNS AND COMBINATIONS.

THIS BOOK IS BASED ON THE NOTES I HAVE COLLECTED FOR MY OWN USE. I HAVE WRITTEN DOWN MY OBSERVATIONS AND COMMENTED AT GREATER LENGTH ON AREAS THAT MY STUDENTS REPEATEDLY QUESTION OR HAVE TROUBLE WITH. THE PATTERNS WITHIN THESE PAGES REPRESENT MANY OF THE MOST COMMONLY SEEN WITH A FEW ADDITIONS THAT MIGHT ONLY BE SEEN ONCE. THERE ARE MANY, MANY MORE PATTERNS TO BE SEEN AND DOCUMENTED. FOR NOW, I HOPE THAT THOSE OF YOU ATTRACTED TO THE WONDERFUL QUILTS OF THESE GENTLE PEOPLE WILL BE ABLE TO MAKE GOOD USE OF THE PATTERNS WITHIN THIS BOOK.

I ENCOURAGE YOU TO FOLLOW IN THE FOOTSTEPS OF OUR AMISH FRIENDS AND EXPLORE NEW POSSIBILITIES IN QUILT DESIGN. FOR MANY, THE PATTERNS IN THIS BOOK WILL PROVIDE A NEW DIRECTION REQUIRING YOU TO SET ASIDE PRE-CONCEIVED NOTIONS OF WHAT "GOES TOGETHER". FOR ME, IT IS THIS STEPPING OUT AND STRETCHING PROCESS THAT HAS PROVIDED NEW GROWTH IN MY QUILTMAKING. MISTAKES WILL BE MADE BUT YOUR SUCCESSES WILL INSPIRE YOU ON. I HOPE THIS BOOK, WITH ITS INFORMATION, PATTERNS AND IDEAS WILL PROVIDE AN ADDITIONAL AVENUE FOR YOUR CREATIVITY.

> *" Whatsoever thy hand findeth to do,*
> *do it with thy might."*
> *Ecclesiastes 9:10*

CHAPTER ONE
COLOR

COLOR IS THE KEY INGREDIENT TO THE LIFE ONE FEELS WHEN VIEWING
AN AMISH QUILT. IT IS ALSO AN AREA THAT CAN CAUSE THE GREATEST
FRUSTRATION TO BEGINNING QUILTMAKERS. THE AMISH QUILTER HAD A
DISTINCT ADVANTAGE IN THAT HER COLOR PALETTE WAS LIMITED TO
FABRICS ON HAND. OUR PALETTE IS UNLIMITED AND CHOOSING IS FURTHER
COMPLICATED BY EASY AVAILABILITY.

EARLY AMISH QUILTS WERE OFTEN MADE FROM SCRAPS AND PIECES OF FABRIC
LEFT OVER FROM GARMENTS. THE WONDERFULLY SUBTLE SHADES AND HUES
OF RED, BLUE, BROWN AND GREEN WERE A RESULT OF USING DYE STUFFS
THAT GREW NATURALLY AND WERE READILY AVAILABLE IN VARIOUS
GEOGRAPHICAL LOCATIONS PLUS WERE APPROVED BY THE BISHOP OF THE
COMMUNITY FOR USE IN SHIRTS, PANTS, APRONS, DRESSES ETC.   PRINTS
AND STRIPES WERE CONSIDERED WORLDLY AND UNNACCEPTABLE. AS COMMERCIAL
DYES BECAME MORE AVAILABLE, THE ONCE MUTED SHADES OF HAND DYED
CLOTH TOOK ON A BRIGHTER, HARSHER LOOK AND COLORS BECAME AVAILABLE
THAT WERE NOT POSSIBLE TO OBTAIN FROM ORGANIC DYE STUFFS.

DURING THE EARLY 20'S MORE AND MORE OF THE WOOL, COTTON AND LINEN
THAT WAS SPUN, WOVEN AND DYED WITHIN THE COMMUNITY WAS FORSAKEN
FOR "STORE BOUGHT" FABRICS. THESE POLISHED COTTONS, CREPES ETC., IN
BLACK, GREEN, BROWN, PURPLE, RED AND BLUE WERE AVAILABLE IN A
GREAT VARIETY OF SHADES AND INTENSITIES OF COLOR. THE COLORS
CHOSEN FOR MAKING QUILTS DEPENDED IN A LARGE PART ON THE RULES OF
THE COMMUNITY LIVED IN. SOME WERE MORE CONSERVATIVE THAN OTHERS.
THIS RESULTED IN COLORS AND DESIGNS DIFFERING GREATLY FROM ONE
COMMUNITY TO THE NEXT. WHAT APPEARS TO BE A RULE OF THUMB FOR
ONE GROUP MAY NOT BE SO FOR ANOTHER. SOME OLD ORDER COMMUNITIES
STILL ADHERE TO RULINGS FORBIDDING ANYTHING OTHER THAN WHOLE
CLOTH QUILTS.

BLACK IS A COLOR ASSOCIATED WITH THE AMISH. IT IS A BASIC PART
OF THEIR DRESS. BLACK HATS, CAPES, PANTS, STOCKINGS, VESTS,
JACKETS, SHOES ETC. ARE A COMMON SIGHT IN AMISH COMMUNITIES. IT
IS A PRACTICAL COLOR AS IT DOES NOT SHOW WEAR OR SOIL AS READILY
AS OTHER COLORS. CONFORMITY OF DRESS CONTRIBUTES TO THE UNITY
WITHIN THE COMMUNITY AND APPEARS AN OUTWARD STATEMENT OF THE INNER
CONVICTION OF THE EQUALITY OF ALL COMMUNITY INDIVIDUALS. THE
AMISH ARE A NON-COMPETITIVE PEOPLE AND THEIR DRESS AS WELL AS
THEIR LIFESTYLE REFLECTS THIS. AMISH CLOTHING IS A PRACTICAL AND
MODEST BODY COVERING. BLACK, BEING SO PREVALENT DUE TO ITS USE IN
CLOTHING, APPEARS OFTEN WITHIN THEIR QUILTS. THIS USE OF BLACK,
IS ONE INGREDIENT THAT GIVES THE NEON QUALITY TO MANY OF THE AMISH
QUILTS. IT INTENSIFIES AND HEIGHTENS THE COLORS IT IS USED WITH.
MY EXPERIENCE HAS BEEN THAT OFTEN UPON FINISHING A DESIGN AND
WONDERING WHAT WAS MISSING, SOME ACCENTS IN BLACK WILL SPARK WHAT
WOULD OTHERWISE HAVE BEEN AN AVERAGE PIECE. FOR MANY IT IS
DIFFICULT TO THINK OF USING BLACK IN A QUILT, BUT I ENCOURAGE
YOU TO TRY IT IF ONLY IN PEN AND PENCIL ON PAPER TO EXPERIENCE
SOME NEW POSSIBILITIES.

COLOR SUGGESTIONS

I HAVE LISTED SOME COLOR COMBINATIONS COMMONLY SEEN IN AMISH QUILTS, BUT DO ENCOURAGE YOU TO EXPERIMENT ON YOUR OWN. WE, AS QUILTMAKERS, NOW HAVE EVERY COLOR AND SHADE IMAGINABLE AT OUR FINGERTIPS AND OUR PALETTE IS ONLY AS LIMITED AS OUR IMAGINATION. START WITH COLORS YOU ENJOY. I HAVE A WHITE WALL THAT I PIN SCRAPS OF FABRIC ONTO. I SOMETIMES TAKE SEVERAL COLORS I FEEL DRAWN TO AND PUT THEM UP, THEN LIVE WITH THEM FOR AWHILE. SOMETIMES I NEED TO ADD A COLOR AND SOMETIMES TAKE ONE AWAY UNTIL I FIND A COMBINATION THAT IS EXCITING TO ME. BE BOLD. ADD SOME COLORS THAT SEEMINGLY DO NOT GO TOGETHER. THIS IS AN EASY WAY TO EXPERIMENT AND OFTEN AN UNPREDICTABLE COMBINATION WILL APPEAR. I OFTEN ADD A COLOR THAT WILL ONLY FIT NEXT TO A PARTICULAR FABRIC. ORDER OF COLORS IS IMPORTANT. IN ONE OF MY PIECES I USED MANY SHADES AND INTENSITIES OF RED. SOME OF THESE REDS LOOKED TERRIBLE NEXT TO ONE ANOTHER SO I HAD TO BE CAREFUL WHERE I PLACED THEM BUT THE FINISHED PIECE WAS PLEASING TO THE EYE.

IN MANY AMISH QUILTS IT WAS COMMON TO USE A COMBINATION OF ONLY 2 OR 3 COLORS. THE VERY PLAIN , LARGE GEOMETRICS OF THE EARLY QUILTS MADE THIS EASY TO DO AND PROVIDED WONDERFUL BACKGROUND SURFACE FOR INTRICATE QUILTING DESIGNS. IT IS THE SIDE BY SIDE PLACEMENT OF THESE COLORS THAT IS SO DYNAMIC, OFTEN ONLY TWO COLORS WITH THE THIRD COLOR BROUGHT IN AS A WIDE BINDING FRAMING THE QUILT.

LEARN TO BE YOUR OWN JUDGE OF COLOR. IT IS EASY TO CREATE FOR APPROVAL BUT USUALLY NOT AS SATISFYING. THERE WILL ALWAYS BE SOMEONE WHO DOESN'T APPROVE OF YOUR COLOR OR DESIGN CHOICES. YOU BE THE JUDGE. CREATIVITY IS A PERSONAL MATTER AND AN EXPRESSION OF WHO YOU ARE. GO WITH WHAT YOU LIKE. YOUR CONFIDENCE WILL INCREASE WITH YOUR BOLDNESS.

SOME AMISH COLOR COMBINATIONS

PEACOCK BLUE, BRIGHT GREEN, DARK BLUE, BLACK
BRIGHT RED, BLUE (PEACOCK, ROYAL OR NAVY)
DEEP RED, DARK GREEN
PURPLE, MAROON, DEEP BLUE
GOLD, BROWN, BLACK
RUST, RED, BROWN
TAN, BROWN, ROYAL BLUE
BLACK, RED, GREEN
DARK GREEN, LIGHT GREEN, BLACK
RED, BROWN, BLACK
MAUVE, DEEP GREEN, DARK RED
BLACK, LIGHT BLUE
LIGHT BLUE, TAN, BLACK
DARK GOLD, BLUE, BLACK
GREEN, MAROON, BLUE, MAUVE

THESE COLORS NEED NOT BE EXACT. EXPERIMENT. THIS LIST IS MEANT ONLY TO PROVIDE THOSE OF YOU WHO DON'T KNOW WHERE TO START, A BEGINNING.

COLORS UNCOMMON TO AMISH QUILTS

WHITE (USUALLY RESERVED FOR FUNERALS), YELLOW AND ORANGE

POSSIBILITIES

IT IS RARE TO FIND PRINTED FABRICS USED IN AMISH QUILTS. HOWEVER, I HAVE DISCOVERED THROUGH TRIAL AND ERROR THAT SOME OF THE LARGE DESIGNER PRINTS AS WELL AS STRIPED SHIRTING FABRIC AVAILABLE TODAY LEND THEMSELVES WELL TO THE BOLD GEOMETRIC DESIGNS OF THE AMISH. (SEE "STAR WITHIN A STAR" ON BACK COVER). MIXED SPARINGLY WITH SOLID FABRICS THEY OFFER AN EXCITING NEW DIMENSION TO THESE CONTEMPORARY DESIGNS. WHEN CHOOSING FABRICS, MY FIRST CHOICE IN FIBER CONTENT IS ALWAYS 100% COTTON. THERE ARE MANY OCCASIONS WHEN PREFERRED FIBER CONTENT MUST BE SACRIFICED TO ACCOMMODATE COLOR NEEDS. YOU MAY EVEN WANT TO TRY USING FABRICS IN A VARIETY OF TEXTURES LIKE VELVET, POLISHED COTTON, SATIN, SILK, WOOLS ETC. EXPERIMENTATION IS FUN AND CAN BE REWARDING.

"She seeks wool and flax,
and works with willing hands.
She is like the ships of the merchant,
she brings her food from afar.
She rises while it is yet night
and provides food for her household
and tasks for her maidens.
She considers a field and buys it;
with the fruit of her hands she
plants a vineyard.
She girds her loins with strength
and her arms are strong.
She perceives that her merchandise
is profitable.
Her lamp does not go out at night.
She puts her hands to the distaff,
and her hands hold the spindle.
She opens her hand to the poor,
and reaches out her hands to the needy.
She is not afraid of snow for her household,
for all her household are clothed in
scarlet.
She makes herself coverings;
her clothing is fine linen and purple.
Her husband is known in the gates,
when he sits among the elders of the land.
She makes linen garments and sells them;
she delivers girdles to the merchant.
Strength and dignity are her clothing,
and she laughs at the time to come.
She opens her mouth with wisdom,
and the teaching of kindness is on her tongue."

Proverbs 31:13-26

CHAPTER TWO
BORDERS

OUT OF THE PROFOUNDLY STRUCTURED AND ORDERLY LIVES OF THE AMISH
HAVE COME QUILT DESIGNS EQUALLY STRUCTURED AND ORDERLY. AMISH
QUILTS ARE OFTEN CONFINED BY SOME SORT OF BORDER OF WHICH THE
COMBINATIONS OF THESE MAY VARY GREATLY. THE BORDER SOMETIMES
SURROUNDS A SOLID PIECE OF FABRIC OR A LARGE PIECED GEOMETRIC
DESIGN MAKING THIS BORDER, PIECED OR PLAIN, THE FOCAL POINT. THE
OUTER BORDERS ARE OFTEN THE WIDTH OF A SINGLE BLOCK, TEN INCHES
OR EVEN WIDER.

THE EARLIEST AMISH QUILTS WERE SIMPLY WHOLE PIECES OF CLOTH
QUILTED TOGETHER, OFTEN WITH A WIDE CONTRASTING BINDING.
THE FRAMED MEDALLIONS MAY HAVE COME FROM A NEED TO BETTER USE
CLOTHING REMNANTS RESULTING IN THE BIRTH OF THE CENTER DIAMOND
AND BARS VARIATIONS. ELABORATE PIECING WAS OFTEN CONSIDERED
PRIDEFUL AND UNNECESSARY, BUT QUILTING MOTIFS WERE INTRICATE
AND GRACEFUL. WIDE BORDERS AND LARGE DESIGN AREAS GAVE AMPLE
OPPORTUNITY TO THE QUILTER TO EXERCISE HER SKILL WITH A
NEEDLE. THE WIDE OUTSIDE BORDERS EVENTUALLY DEVELOPED TO
SURROUND AN INNER BORDER AND LATER, AN ELABORATED INNER BORDER.
CORNER SQUARES PROVIDED ADDITIONAL OPPORTUNITY FOR COLOR AND
DESIGN.

THE DESIGN FORMS OF AMISH BORDERS ARE PERFECT FOR SIMPLE
CONSTRUCTING AND FIGURING. I HAVE NOT SEEN ANY MITERED CORNERS
AS YET. RATHER, THE CORNERS ARE BUTTED UP TO ONE ANOTHER WHERE
THEY MEET. THESE LINES LEND THEMSELVES WELL TO MACHINE SEWING
AS WELL AS SIMPLE BUILD AS YOU GO CONSTRUCTION.

THE TWELVE BORDER VARIATIONS PICTURED ON THE NEXT TWO PAGES ARE
A SAMPLING OF SOME OF THE BORDER DESIGNS FOUND ON AMISH QUILTS.
THERE ARE MANY OTHERS, BUT THESE SHOULD HELP AID YOU IN
DESIGNING AND PERHAPS SPARK AN IDEA OF YOUR OWN. THE PROPORTIONS
ILLUSTRATED ARE TYPICAL OF AMISH BORDERS, BUT WHEN DESIGNING
YOUR OWN THERE NEED BE NO ABSOLUTES. THE QUILT PATTERNS IN
THIS BOOK ALREADY HAVE BORDER MEASUREMENTS BUT DO NOT FEEL
LOCKED INTO USING THEM IF YOU FEEL INSPIRED TO TRY SOMETHING
DIFFERENT.

AMISH QUILTS ARE OFTEN SQUARE AND FULL SIZE QUILTS CAN AVERAGE
70 TO 80 INCHES A SIDE. USE THE BORDER DESIGNS ILLUSTRATED WITH
TRACING PAPER AND COLORED PENCILS TO EXPERIMENT WITH A VARIETY
OF COLOR COMBINATIONS. ALTHOUGH THE PIECED STRUCTURE MAY REMAIN
THE SAME, THE VISUAL DESIGN CAN BE RADICALLY CHANGED BY COLOR
CHOICE.

*"She looketh well to the ways of
her household, and eateth not the
bread of idleness."*
Proverbs 31:27

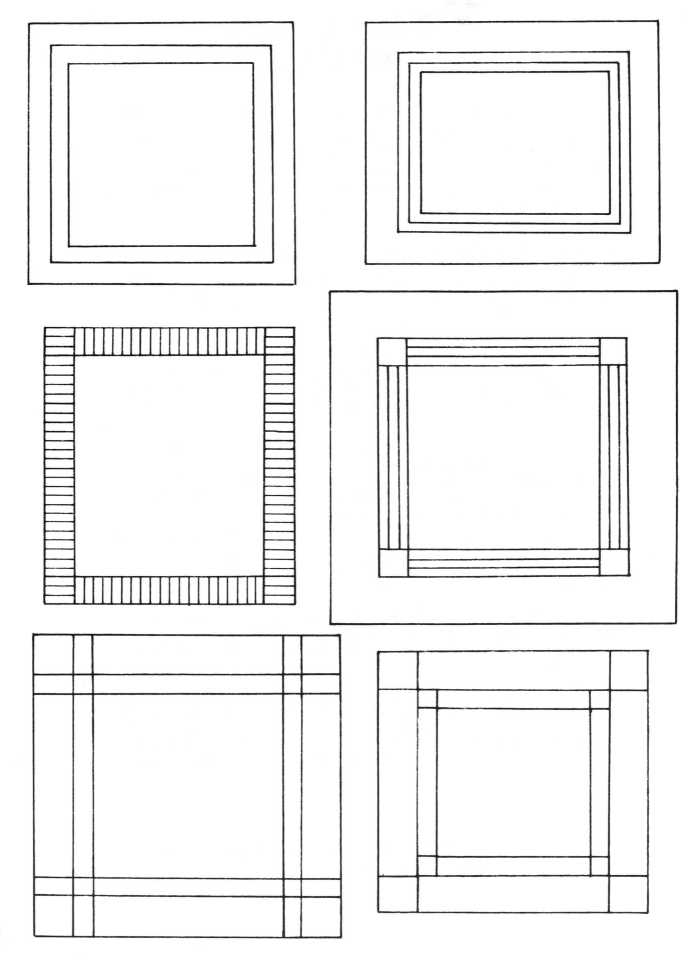

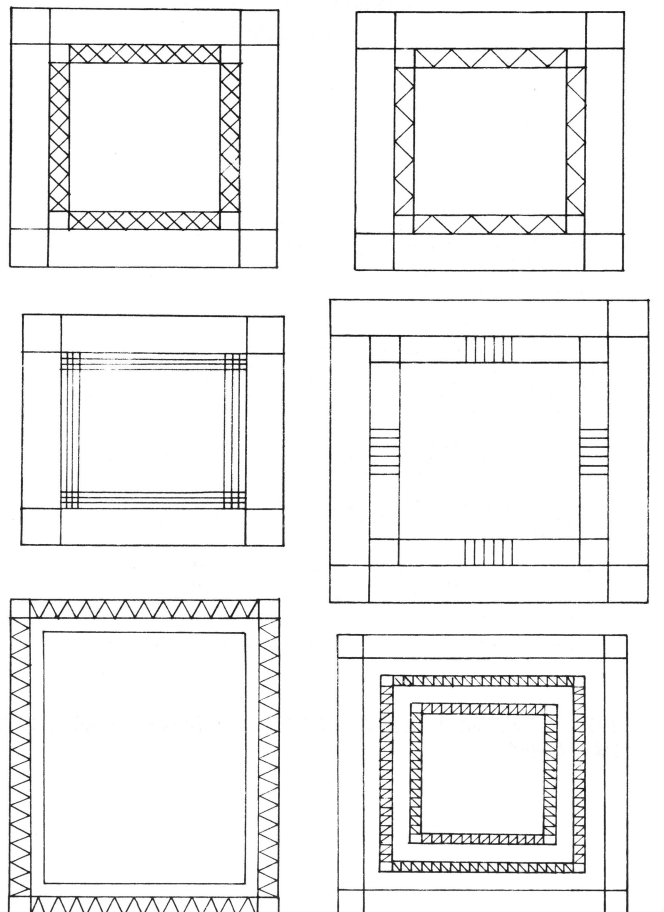

CHAPTER THREE
PATTERNS

AMISH QUILT DESIGNS CONSIST MAINLY OF SQUARES, DIAMONDS, TRIANGLES
AND RECTANGLES WITH VARIATIONS OF THESE. THE DESIGN IS USUALLY
NON-REPRESENTATIONAL CONSISTING OF A TOTALLY GEOMETRIC FORMAT.
THE GEOMETRIC SHAPES MAY TAKE THE FORM OF BASKETS OR STARS, BUT
ONE RARELY SEES APPLIQUE OR CURVED WORK.

WHILE DRAFTING THE PATTERNS OFFERED IN THIS BOOK, I TRIED TO
REMAIN WITHIN THE ORIGINAL CONCEPT, AS I HAVE SEEN IT, AS MUCH
AS POSSIBLE. THE MEASUREMENTS AND SIZES OF LATTICE STRIPS AND
BORDERS CAN BE CHANGED OR ADDED TO AS DECIDED UPON BY THE MAKER.
MIXING AND MATCHING WILL RESULT IN UNIQUE EXPRESSIONS, EACH QUILT
BECOMING AN ORIGINAL. I ENCOURAGE YOU TO CREATE A QUILT USING YOUR
OWN COMBINATIONS.

EACH PATTERN PROVIDES YOU WITH A SCALE DRAWING OF THE FINISHED
QUILT. YOU CAN USE TRACING PAPER AND COLORED PENCILS TO EXPERIMENT
WITH YOUR OWN COLOR COMBINATIONS.

WHEN WORKING WITH BLOCKS, I CUT THE FABRIC FOR ONE AND LAY IT OUT
TO MAKE SURE I AM HAPPY WITH MY COLOR ARRANGEMENT. OFTEN, IT IS AT
THIS STAGE OF THE QUILT THAT I BEGIN MAKING CHANGES.

ALTHOUGH YOU CAN GET SOME IDEA OF THE COLOR YOU WANT TO USE FROM
PENCILING IN THE DESIGN, THE ACTUAL FABRIC IS QUITE DIFFERENT
AND THE COLOR MUCH MORE INTENSE AND TRUE. STAY FLEXIBLE AND BE
YOUR OWN JUDGE.

I HAVE OCCASIONALLY ADDED COMMENTS AND HINTS TO PATTERNS WHERE
I HAVE FELT IT WOULD BE HELPFUL.

ADD ¼″ SEAM ALLOWANCES TO *ALL* MEASUREMENTS AND PATTERNS.

CENTER DIAMOND WALL QUILT — 46½″ X 46½″

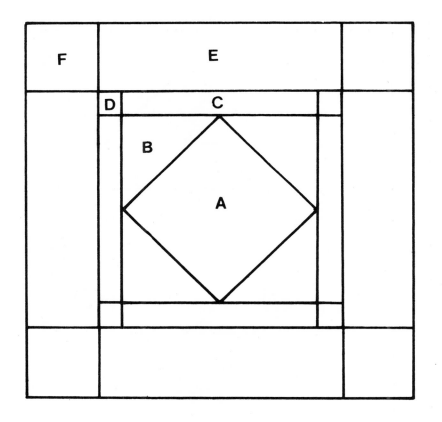

A -16″ X 16″

B - 16″ / 11¼″ / 11¼″

C - 22½″ X 4″

D - 4″ X 4″

E - 8″ X 30½″

F - 8″ X 8″

CENTER DIAMOND VARIATION — 68½″ X 68½″

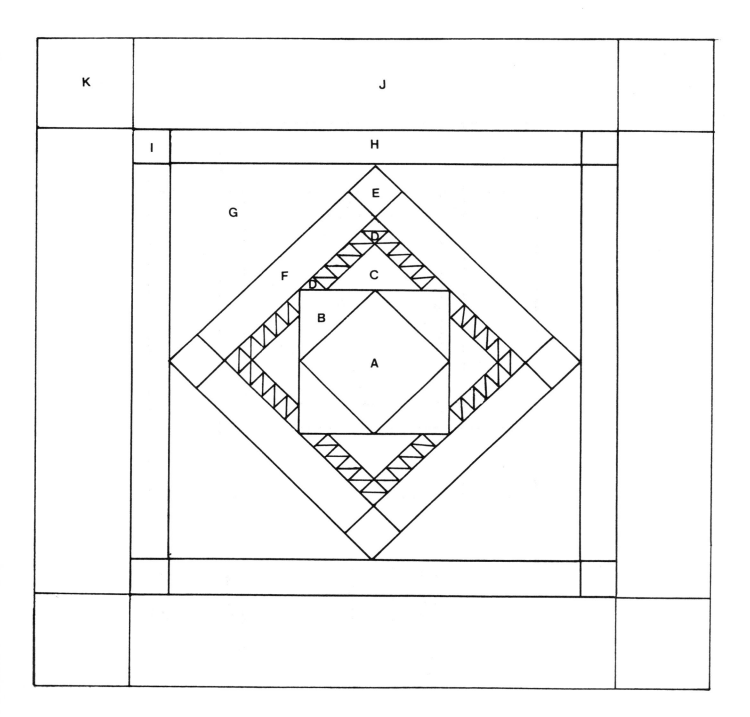

A- 12" X 12"

B- 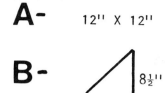 8½"
8½"

C-  8"
8"

H- 42½" X 3"

J- 48½" X 10"

K- 10" X 10"

F- 24" X 3"

G- 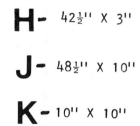 30" 21¼"
21¼"

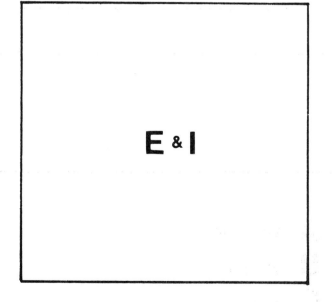

E & I

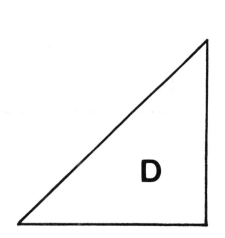

D

CENTER SQUARE — 58″ × 58″

A	24″ X 24″
B	24″ X 6″
C	6″ X 6″
D	36″ X 11″
E	11″ X 11″

BARS VARIATION 1 — 44″ X 64″

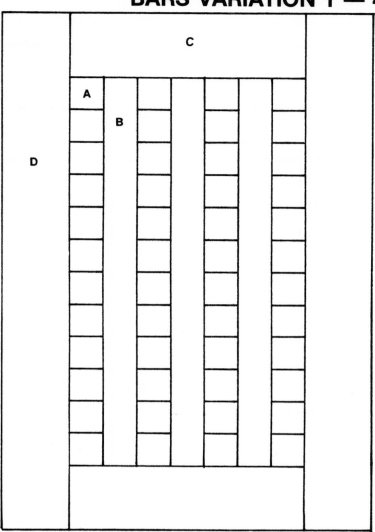

B– 4″ X 48″

C– 8″ X 28″

D– 8″ X 64″

A

19

BARS VARIATION 2 — 64″ X 64″

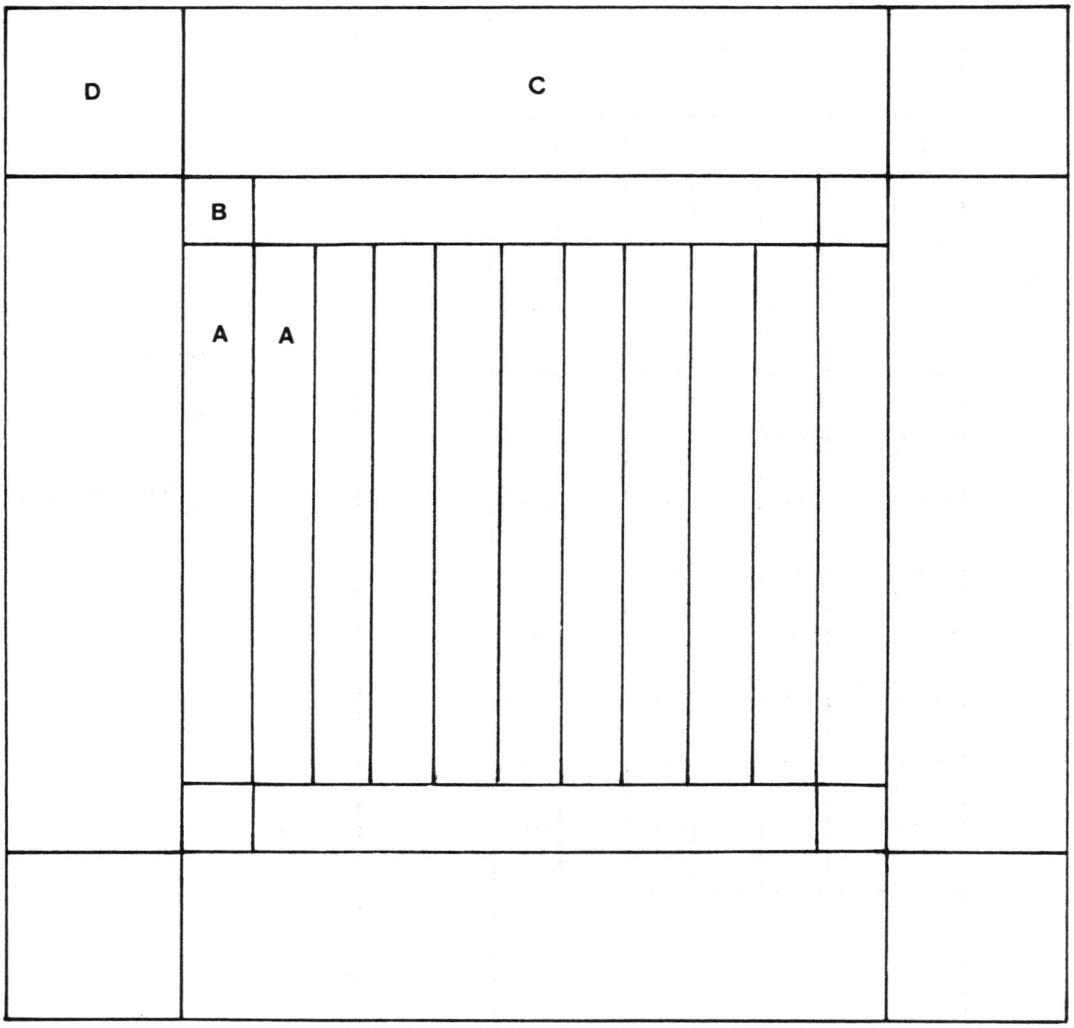

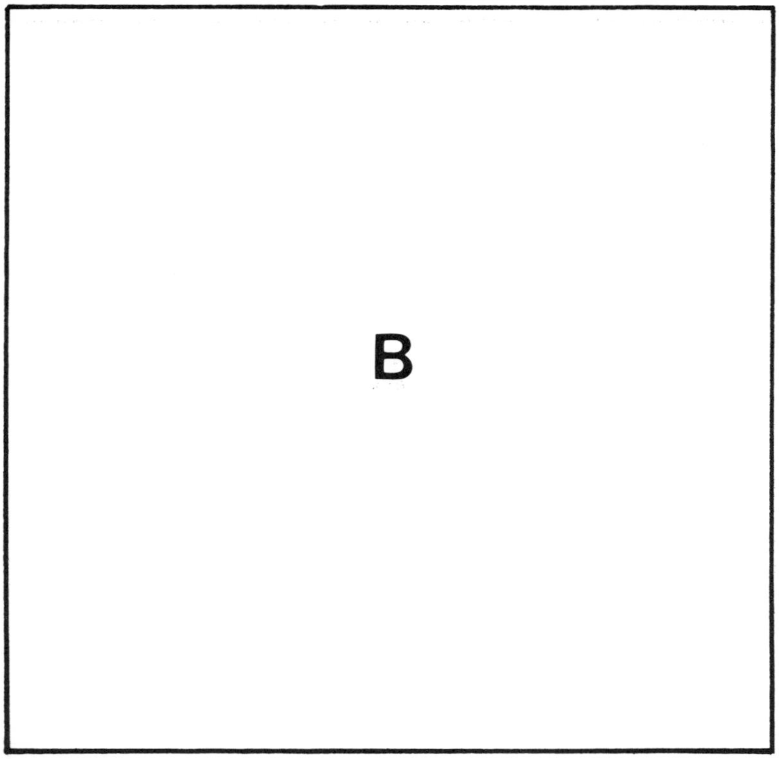

A- 4″ X 36″

C- 10″ X 44″

D- 10″ X 10″

BARS VARIATION 3 — 45″ X 45″

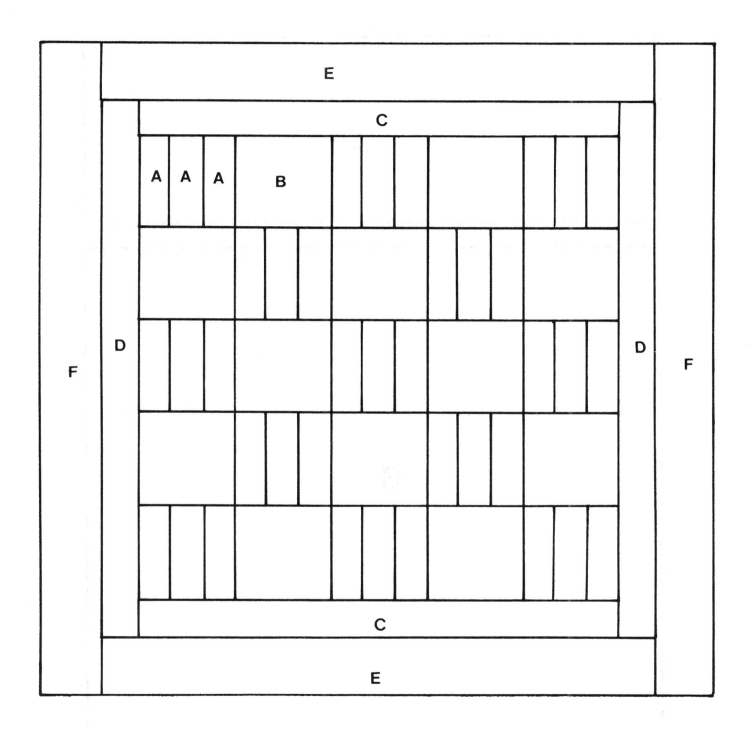

C – 2½'' X 30''   **E** – 5'' X 35''

D – 2½'' X 35''   **F** – 5'' X 45''

A

B

BARS VARIATION 4 — 74½″ X 74½″

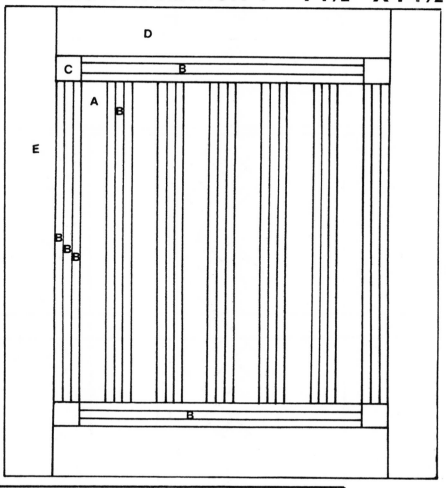

A $4\frac{1}{2}$″   X $49\frac{1}{2}$″

B $1\frac{1}{2}$″   X $49\frac{1}{2}$″

D   8″   X $58\frac{1}{2}$″

E   8″   X $74\frac{1}{2}$″

9 PATCH BARS — 61½″ X 74½″

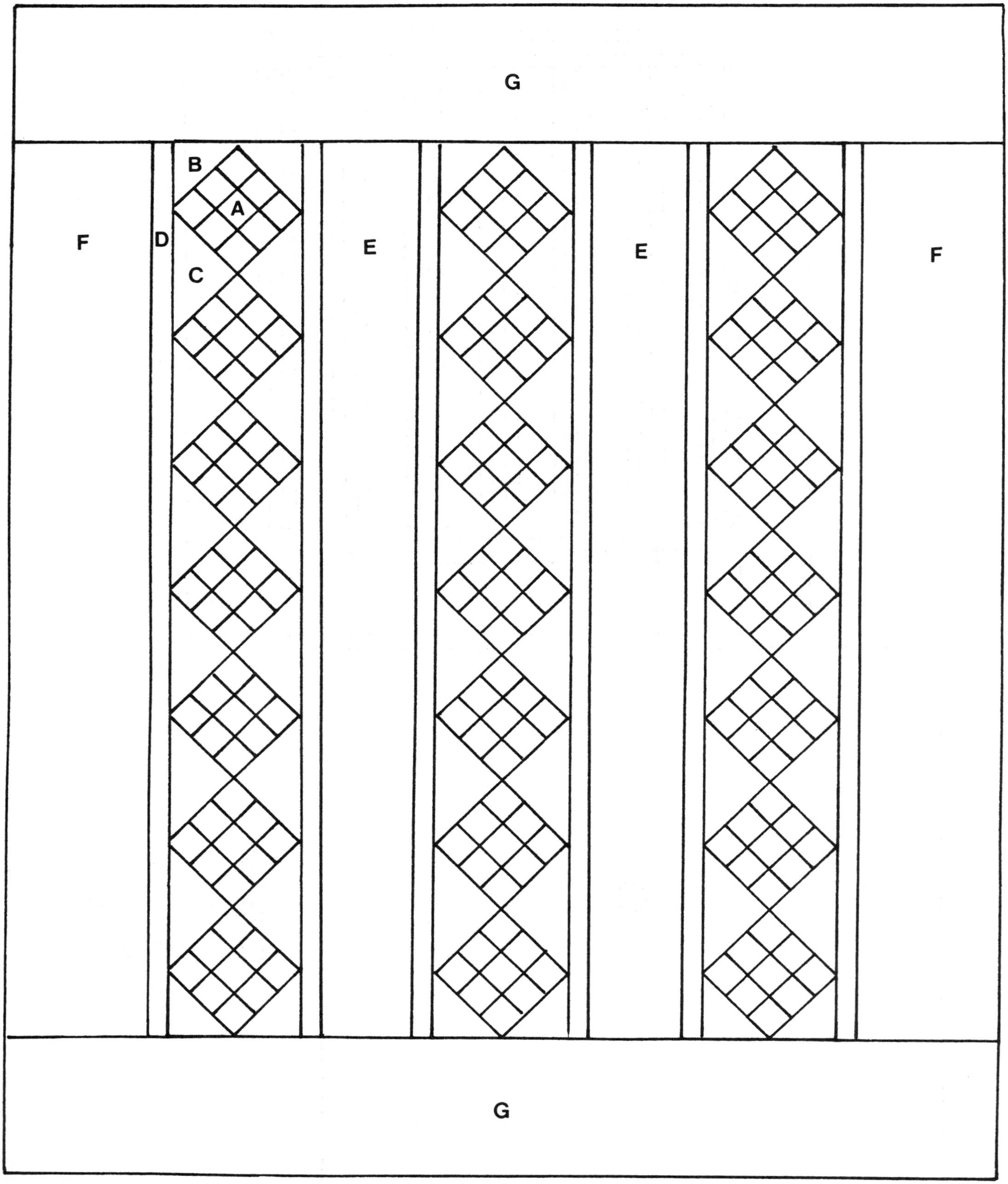

G

B
A
F
D
C
E
E
F

G

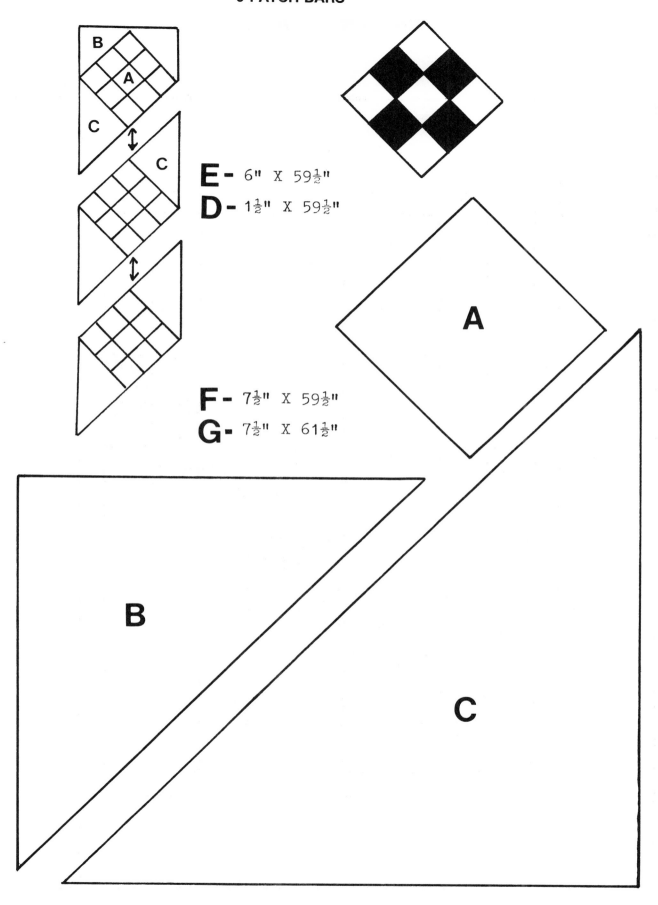

E- 6" X 59½"

D- 1½" X 59½"

F- 7½" X 59½"

G- 7½" X 61½"

BRICKS — 68″ X 56″

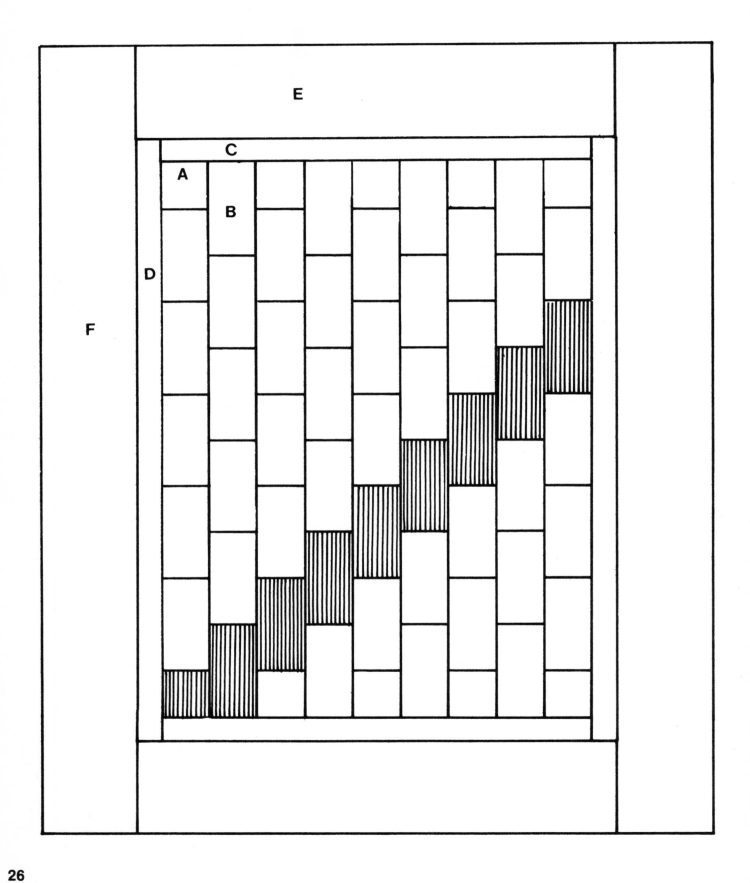

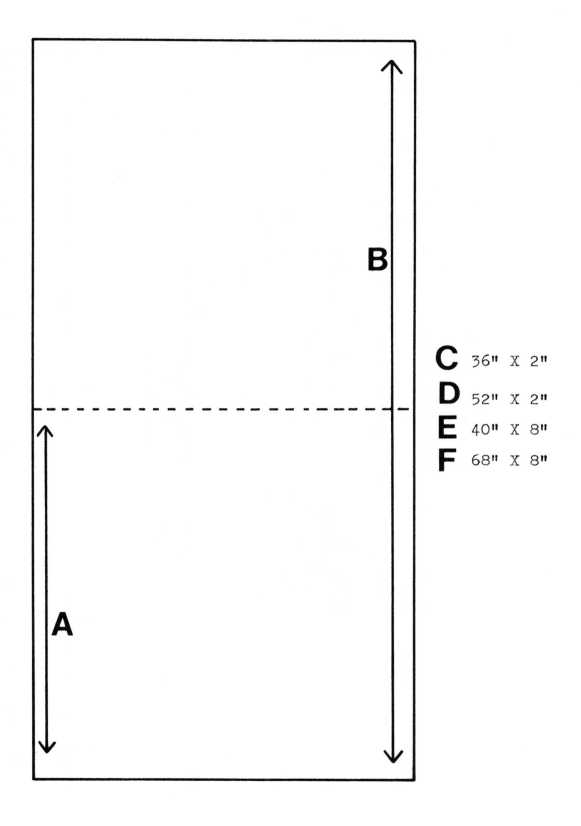

C 36" X 2"

D 52" X 2"

E 40" X 8"

F 68" X 8"

ONE PATCH — 70¼" X 61¾"

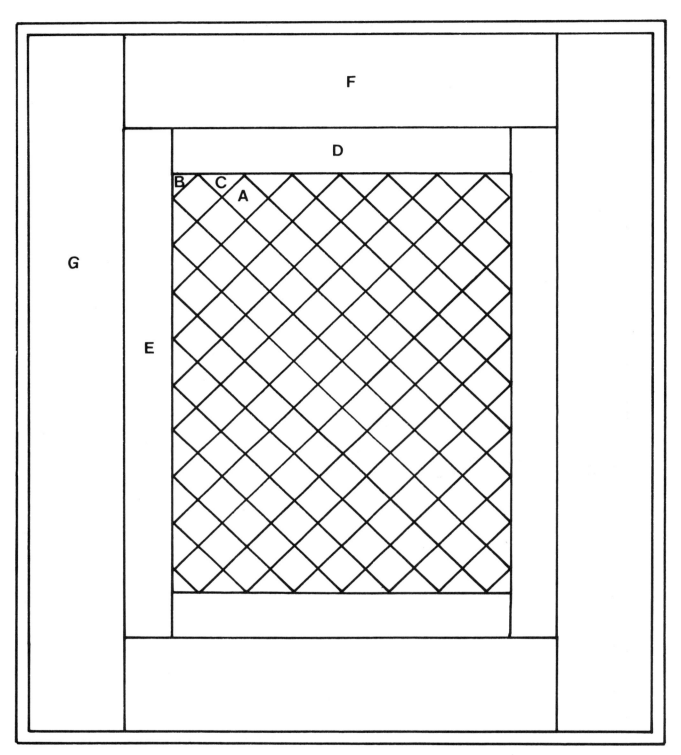

A WIDE BINDING COMPLIMENTS THIS QUILT DESIGN.

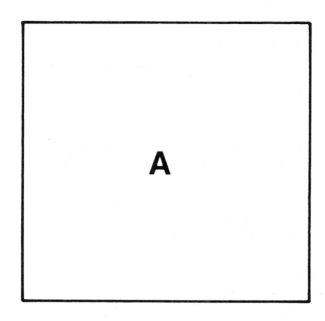

A

D 29 3/4" X 5"

E 48 1/4" X 5"

F 39 3/4" X 11"

G 70 1/4" X 11"

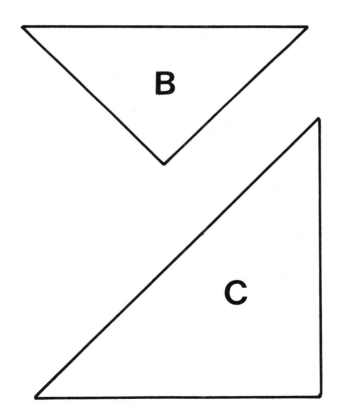

B

C

FOUR PATCH 1 — 89″ X 71″

6″ BLOCK

TRY A WIDE BINDING WITH THIS QUILT.

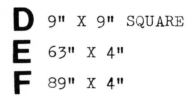

D	9" X 9" SQUARE
E	63" X 4"
F	89" X 4"

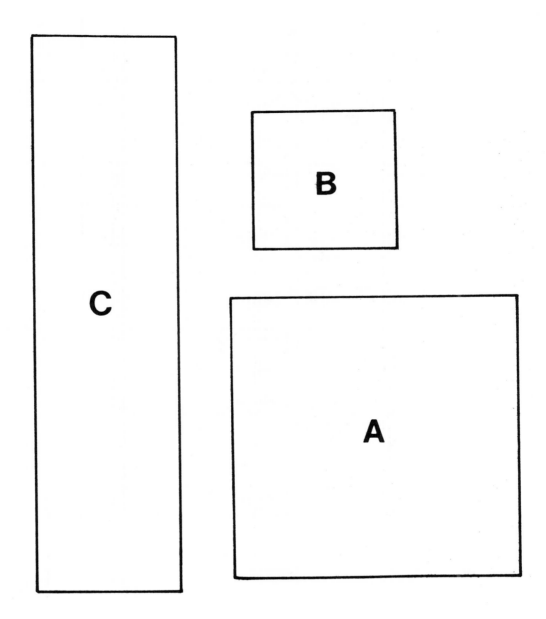

FOUR PATCH 2 — 66¼ " X 54¾ "
4″ BLOCK

FOUR PATCH 2

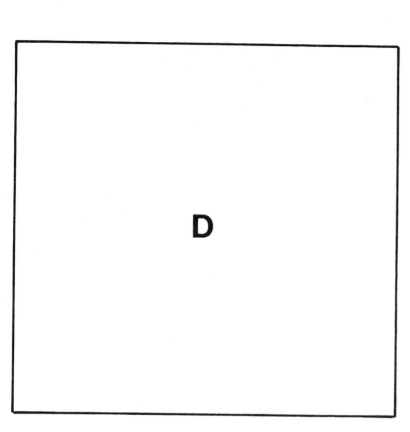

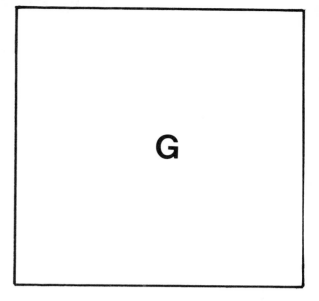

G

D

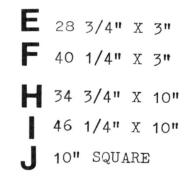

E 28 3/4" X 3"
F 40 1/4" X 3"
H 34 3/4" X 10"
I 46 1/4" X 10"
J 10" SQUARE

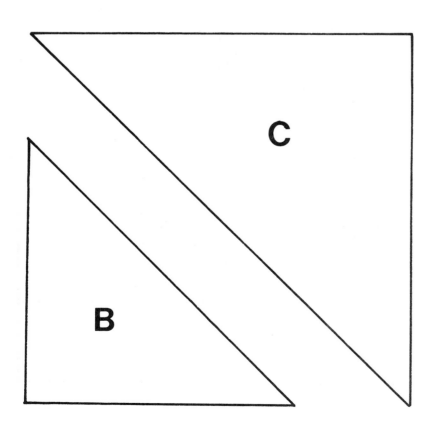

C

B

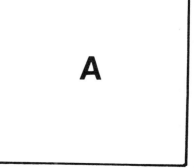

A

33

NINE PATCH — 62½" X 62½"

6" BLOCK

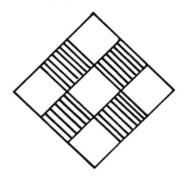

F

E

B
C

A

D

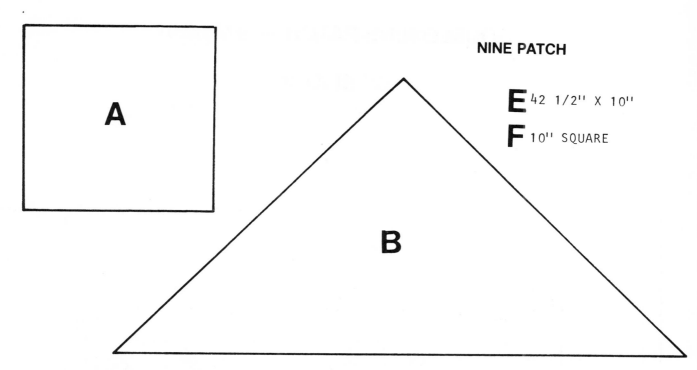

NINE PATCH

E 42 1/2'' X 10''

F 10'' SQUARE

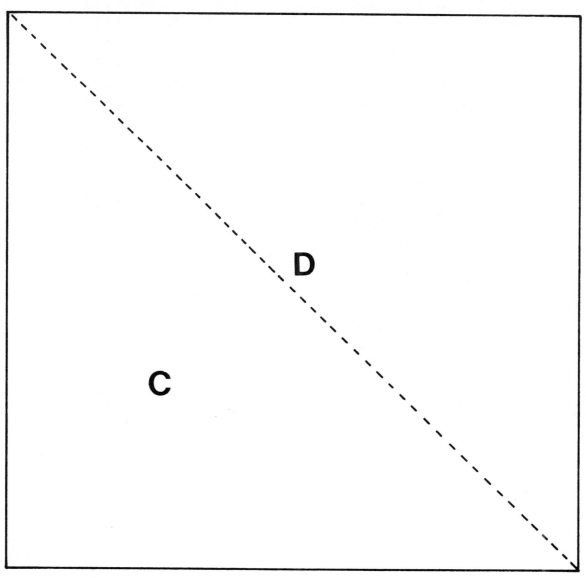

A

B

D

C

DOUBLE NINE PATCH — 97″ X 97″

12″ BLOCK

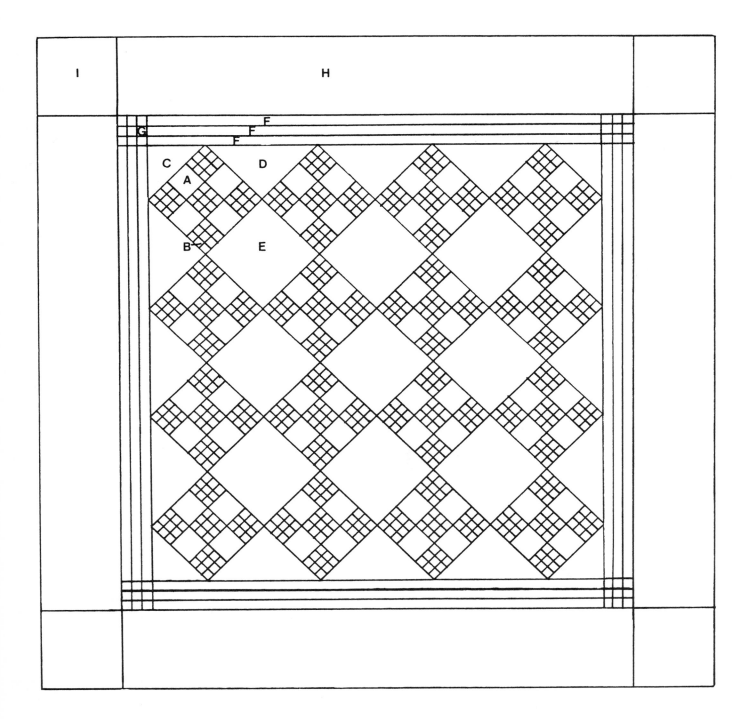

DOUBLE NINE PATCH

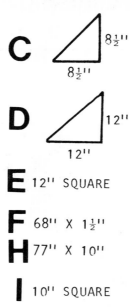

C $8\frac{1}{2}''$ $8\frac{1}{2}''$

D   12''   12''

E 12'' SQUARE

F 68'' X $1\frac{1}{2}''$

H 77'' X 10''

I 10'' SQUARE

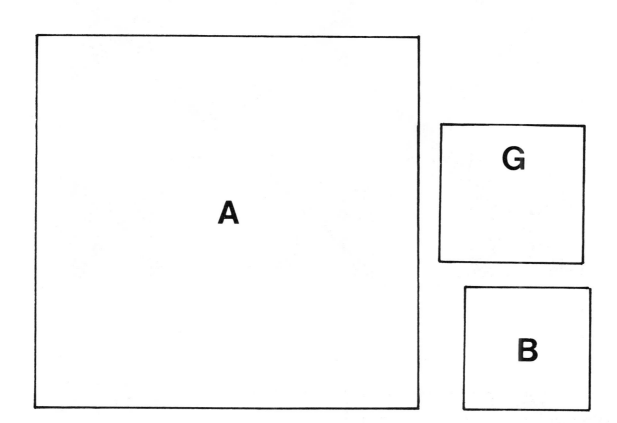

A

G

B

DOUBLE IRISH CHAIN — 71" X 71"
10" BLOCK (SEE FRONT COVER PHOTO)

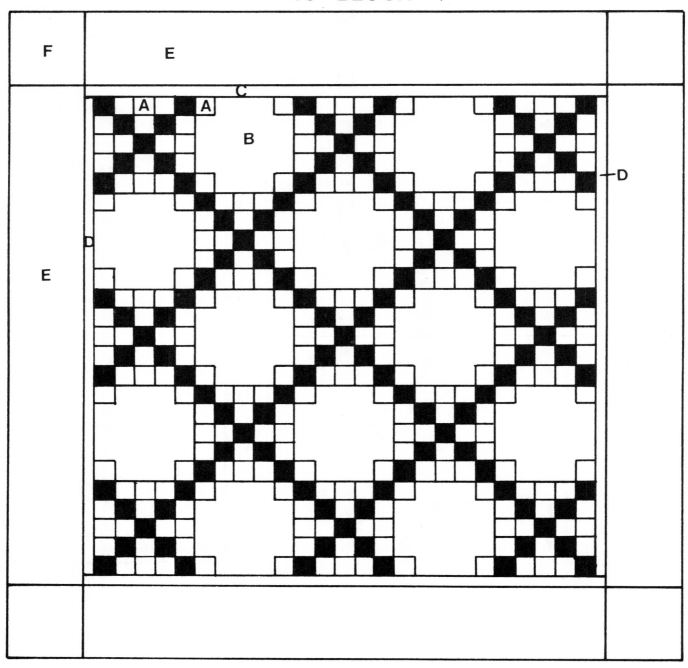

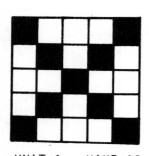

UNIT 1 - MAKE 13

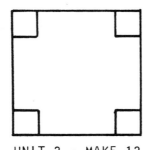

UNIT 2 - MAKE 12

APPLIQUE "A" TO
CORNERS OF THE
10" SQUARE.

A

B 10'' SQUARE

C 53'' X 1 1/2''

D 50'' X 1 1/2''

E 53'' X 9''

F 9'' SQUARE

38

SUNSHINE AND SHADOW 1

SUNSHINE AND SHADOW QUILTS GET THEIR NAME FROM THE
MANY ROWS OF COLOR ALTERNATING LIGHT WITH DARK. THE
BLACKED IN SQUARES AND TRIANGLES ARE THERE TO
ILLUSTRATE THE DIRECTION THE COLORS SHOULD TAKE. THIS
QUILT CAN TAKE ON MANY MOODS DEPENDING ON COLORS USED.

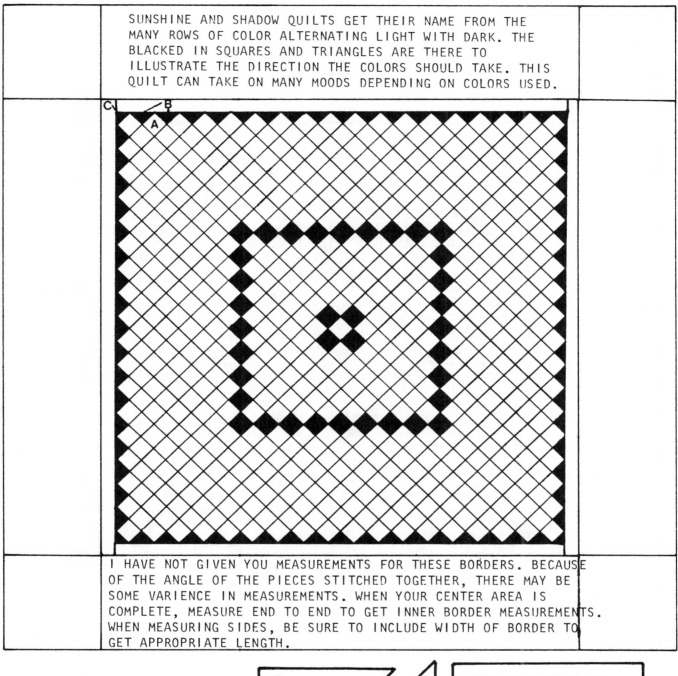

I HAVE NOT GIVEN YOU MEASUREMENTS FOR THESE BORDERS. BECAUSE
OF THE ANGLE OF THE PIECES STITCHED TOGETHER, THERE MAY BE
SOME VARIENCE IN MEASUREMENTS. WHEN YOUR CENTER AREA IS
COMPLETE, MEASURE END TO END TO GET INNER BORDER MEASUREMENTS.
WHEN MEASURING SIDES, BE SURE TO INCLUDE WIDTH OF BORDER TO
GET APPROPRIATE LENGTH.

PIECING DIAGRAM

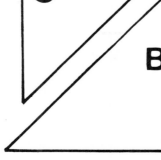

USE THIS TEMPLATE
FOR ALL THREE "S&S"
QUILTS

A

SUNSHINE AND SHADOW 2 — 82″ X 82″

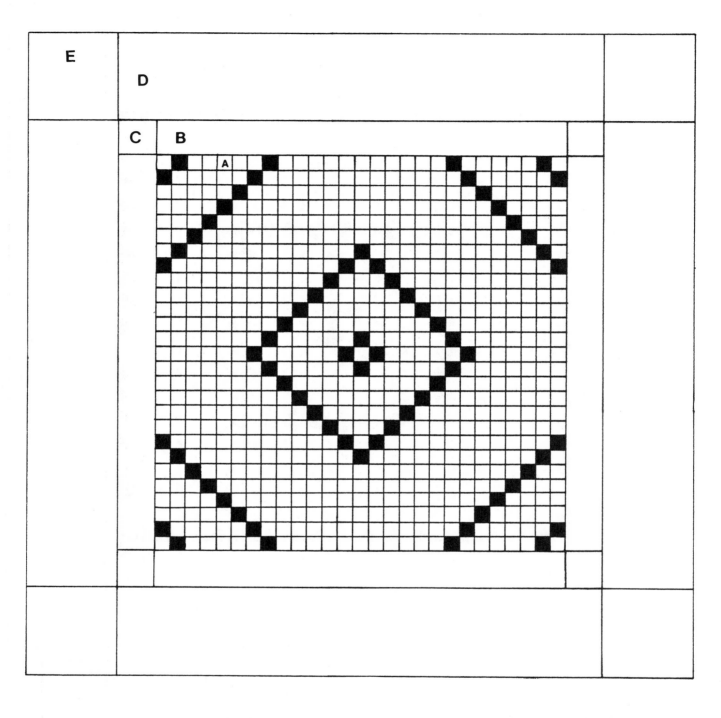

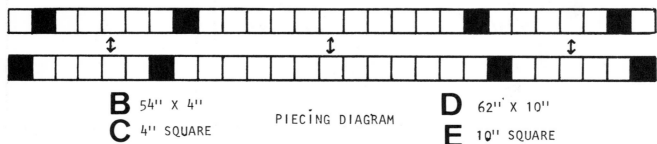

B 54″ X 4″

C 4″ SQUARE

PIECING DIAGRAM

D 62″ X 10″

E 10″ SQUARE

SUNSHINE AND SHADOW 3 — 86″ X 86″

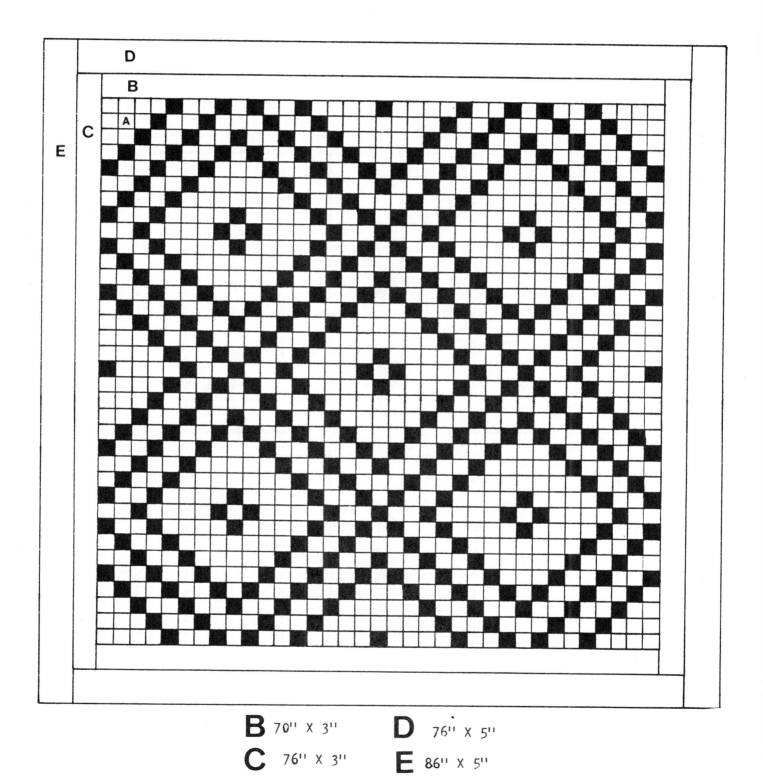

B 70″ X 3″   **D** 76″ X 5″

C 76″ X 3″   **E** 86″ X 5″

SHOO FLY — 61″ X 61″
6″ BLOCK

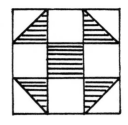

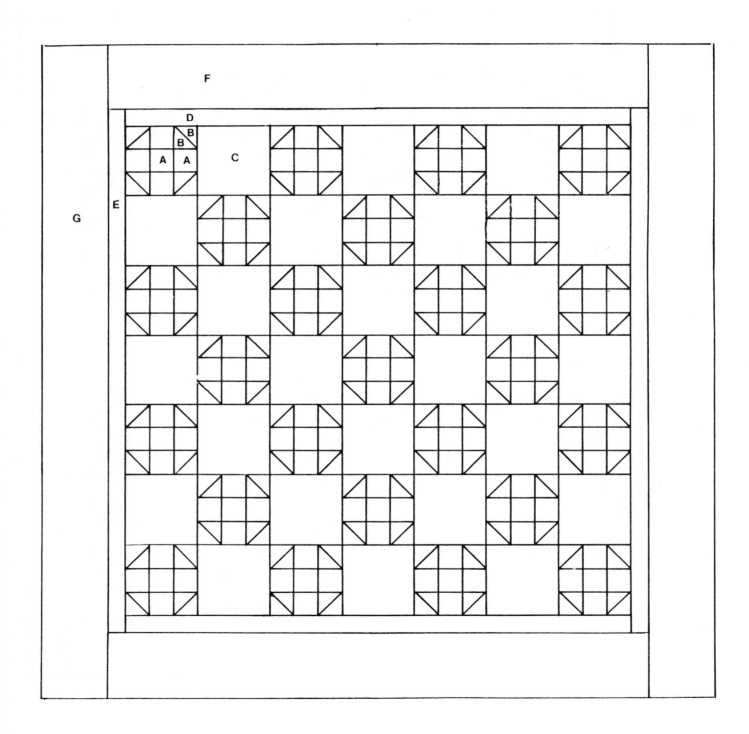

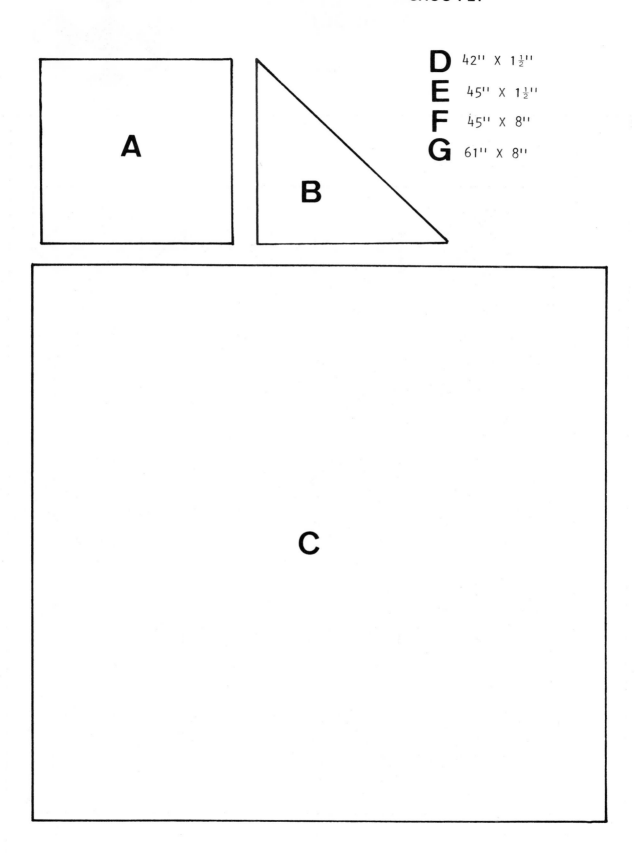

D 42" X 1½"
E 45" X 1½"
F 45" X 8"
G 61" X 8"

FENCE ROW — 79¾" X 67"
9" BLOCK

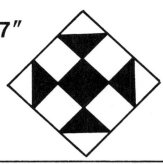

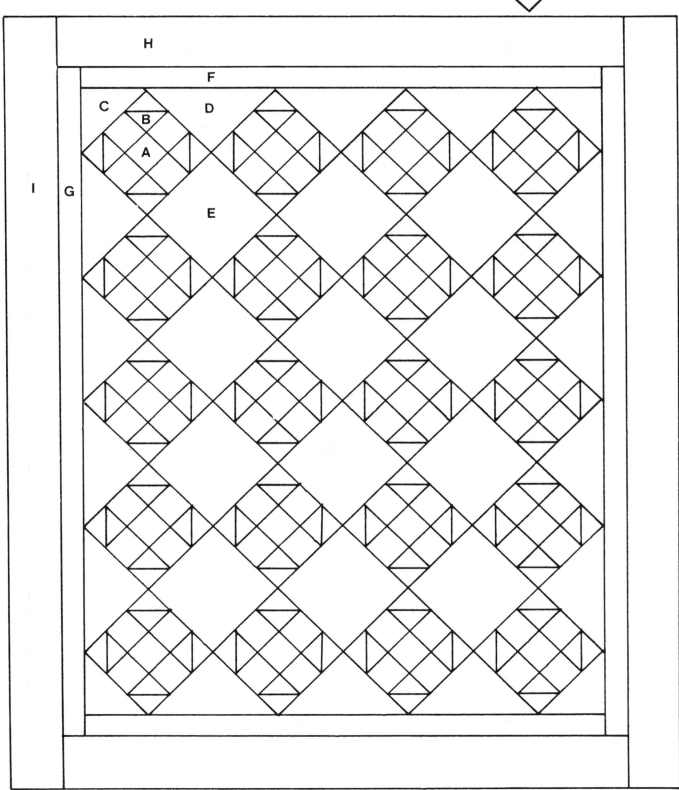

FENCE ROW

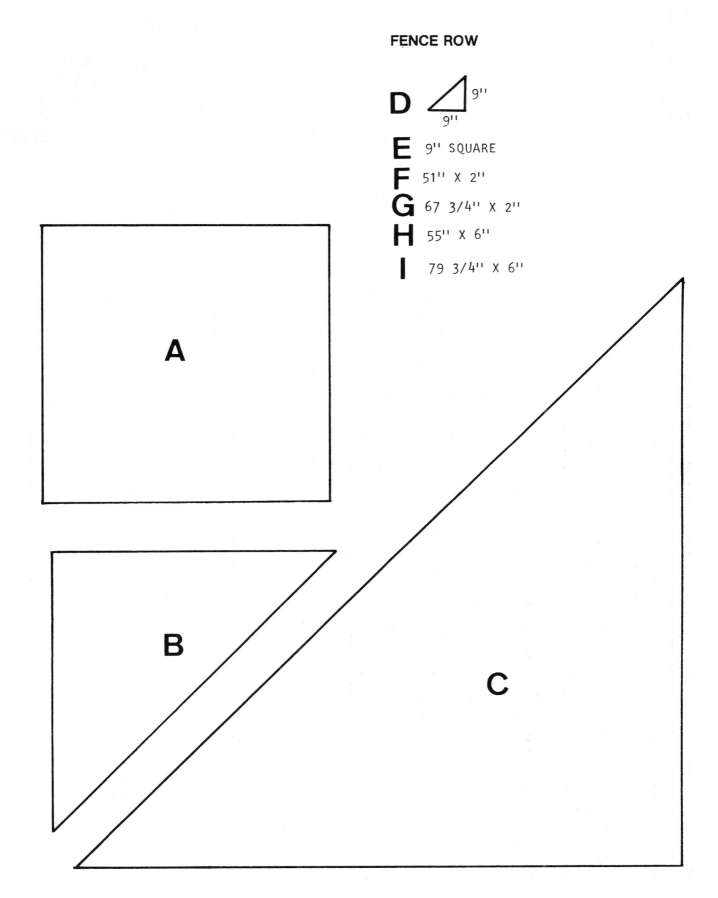

D 9'' / 9''

E 9'' SQUARE

F 51'' X 2''

G 67 3/4'' X 2''

H 55'' X 6''

I 79 3/4'' X 6''

A

B

C

BOW TIE — 84″ X 36″

6″ BLOCK

(SEE BACK COVER PHOTO)

C 24″ X 2″

D 76″ X 2″

E 28″ X 2″

F 80″ X 2″

G 32″ X 2″

H 84″ X 2″

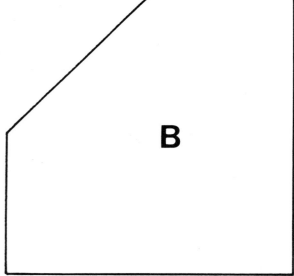

HOLE IN THE BARN DOOR — 83″ X 68¾″

10″ BLOCK

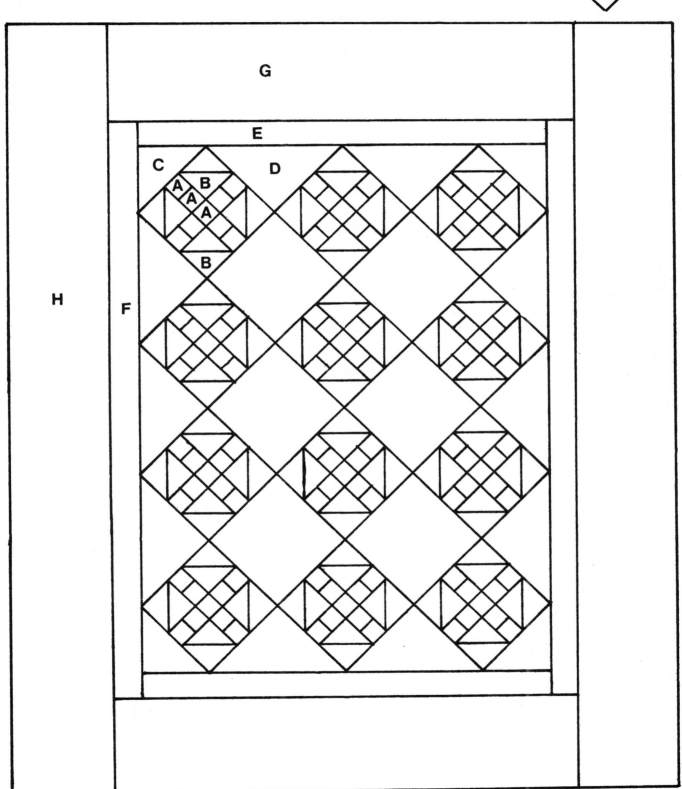

HOLE IN THE BARN DOOR

D 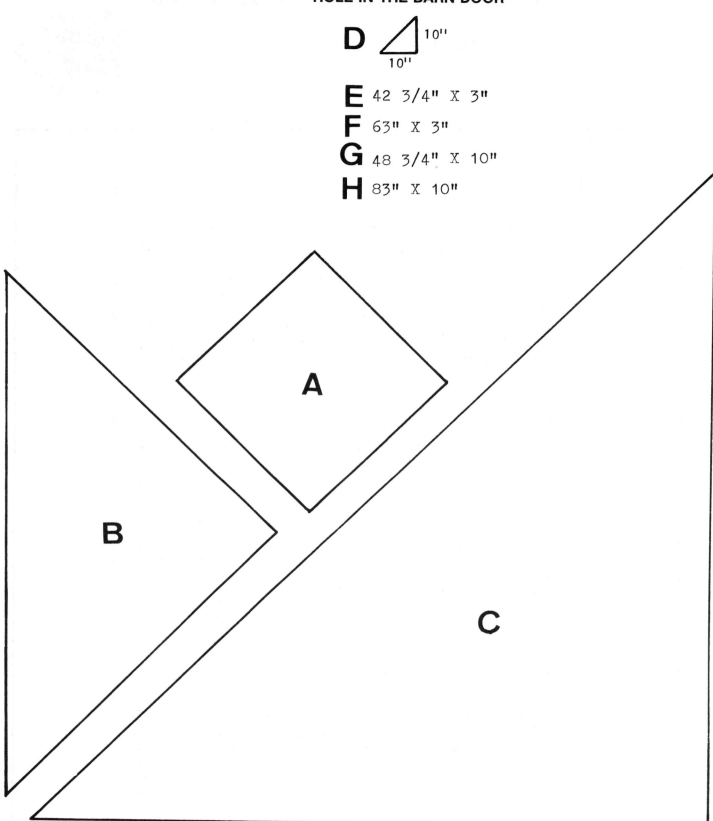 10"
10"

E 42 3/4" X 3"

F 63" X 3"

G 48 3/4" X 10"

H 83" X 10"

DIAMONDS AND SQUARES — 56½" X 56½"
8" BLOCK

BINDING

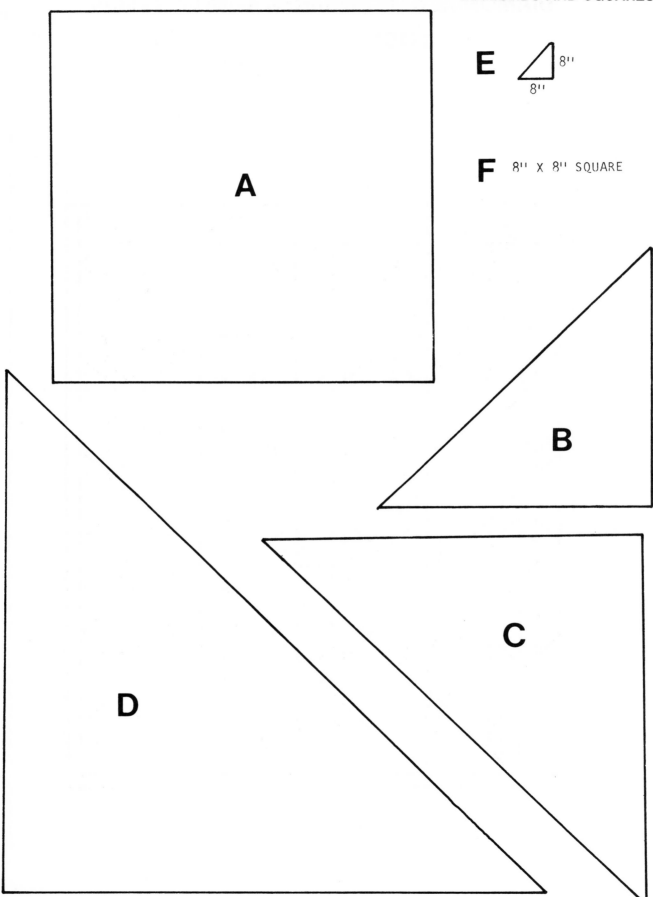

A

E 8''
8''

F 8'' X 8'' SQUARE

B

C

D

CROSS IN THE SQUARE — 64" X 78"

10" BLOCK

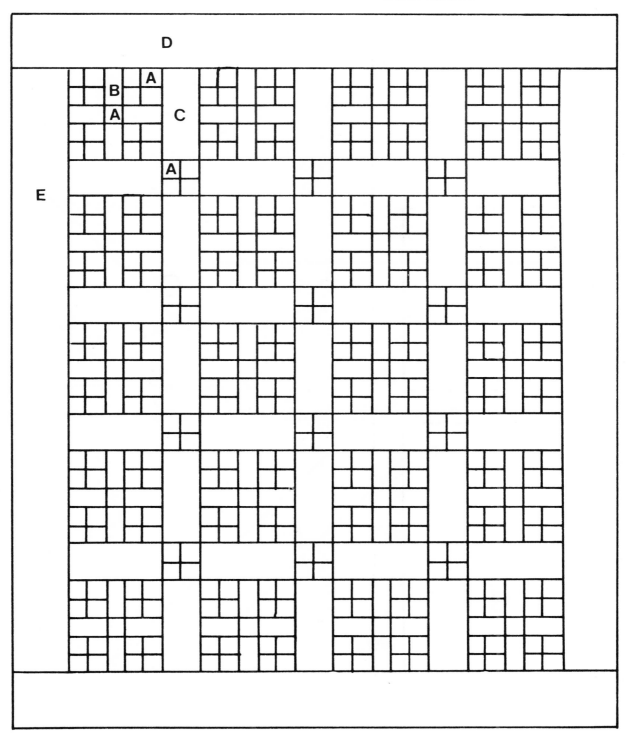

CROSS IN THE SQUARE

D 64'' X 6''
E 66'' X 6''

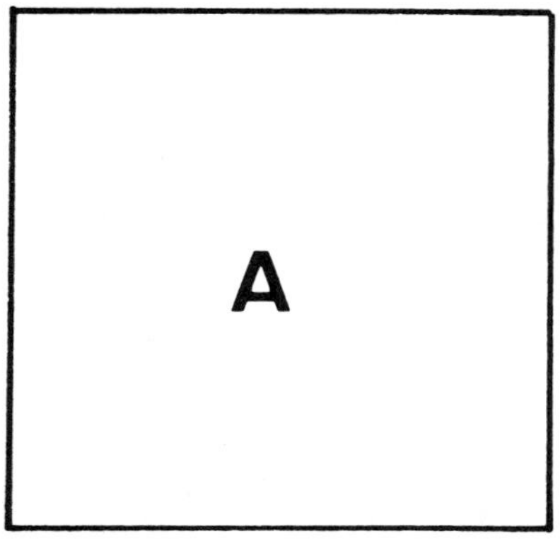

A

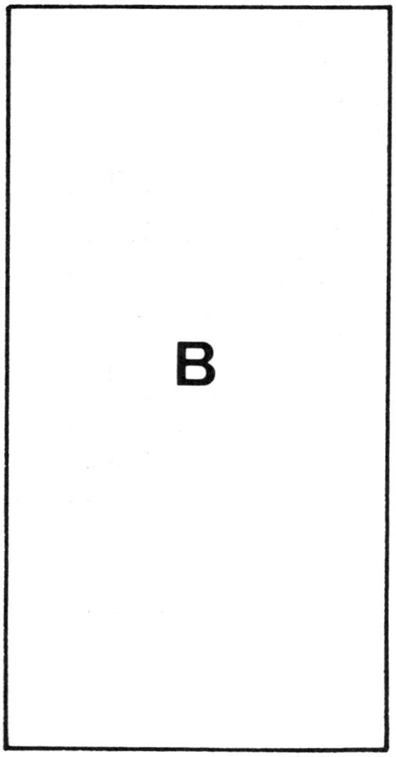

B

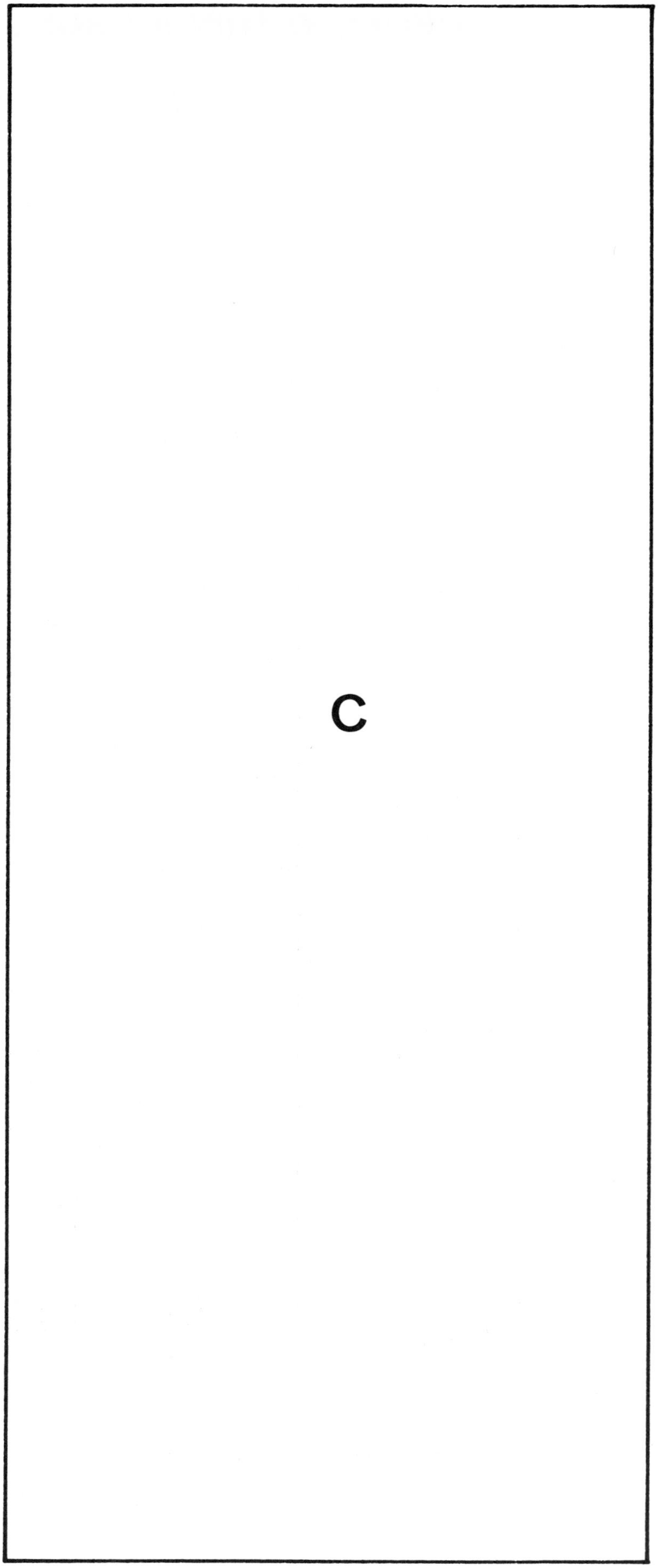

C

CROSS WITHIN A CROSS — 98¾″ X 84⅝″

10″ BLOCK

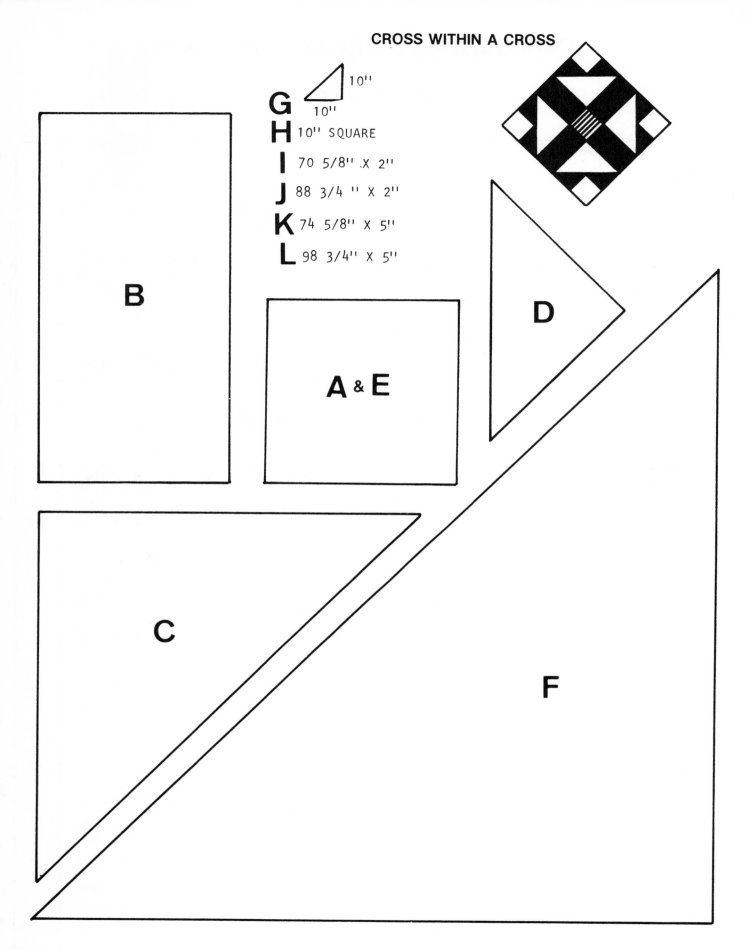

G 10" / 10"

H 10" SQUARE

I 70 5/8" X 2"

J 88 3/4" X 2"

K 74 5/8" X 5"

L 98 3/4" X 5"

B

A & E

D

C

F

BOTCH HANDLE — 99″ X 83″
12″ BLOCK

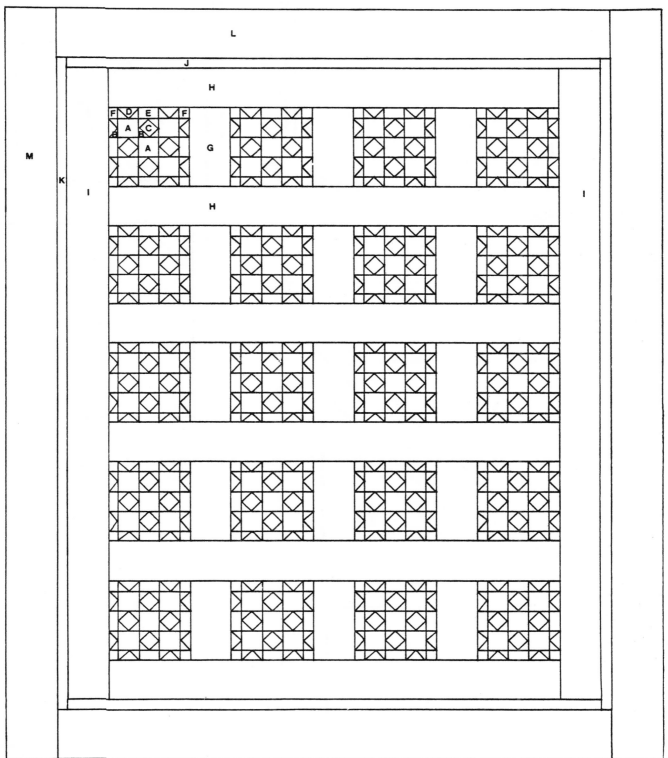

BOTCH HANDLE

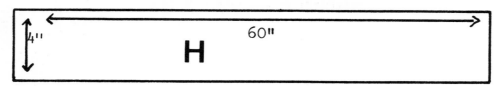

H

60"

4"

LONG LATTICE STRIPS - CUT 6

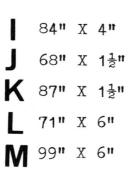

SHORT SIDE LATTICE - CUT 15

G

4"

12"

I 84" X 4"

J 68" X 1½"

K 87" X 1½"

L 71" X 6"

M 99" X 6"

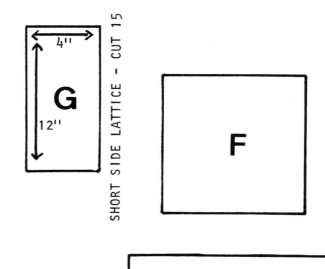

F

C

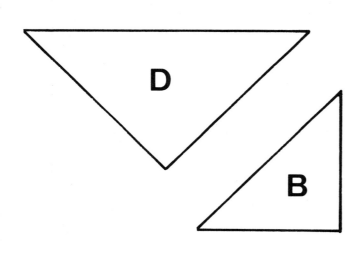

D

B

A

E

BEAR PAW — 99" X 82"
12" BLOCK

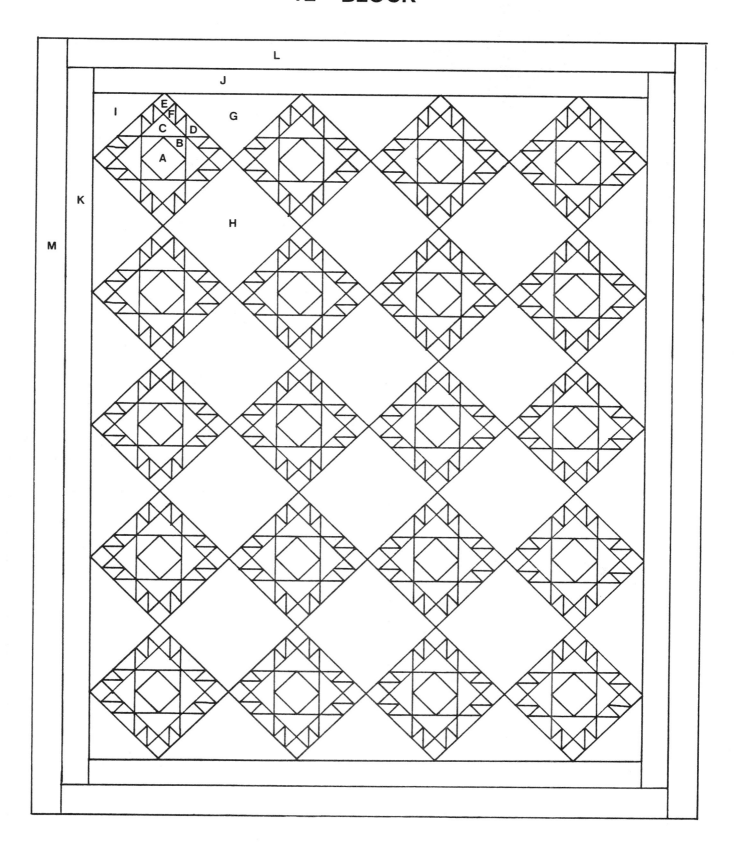

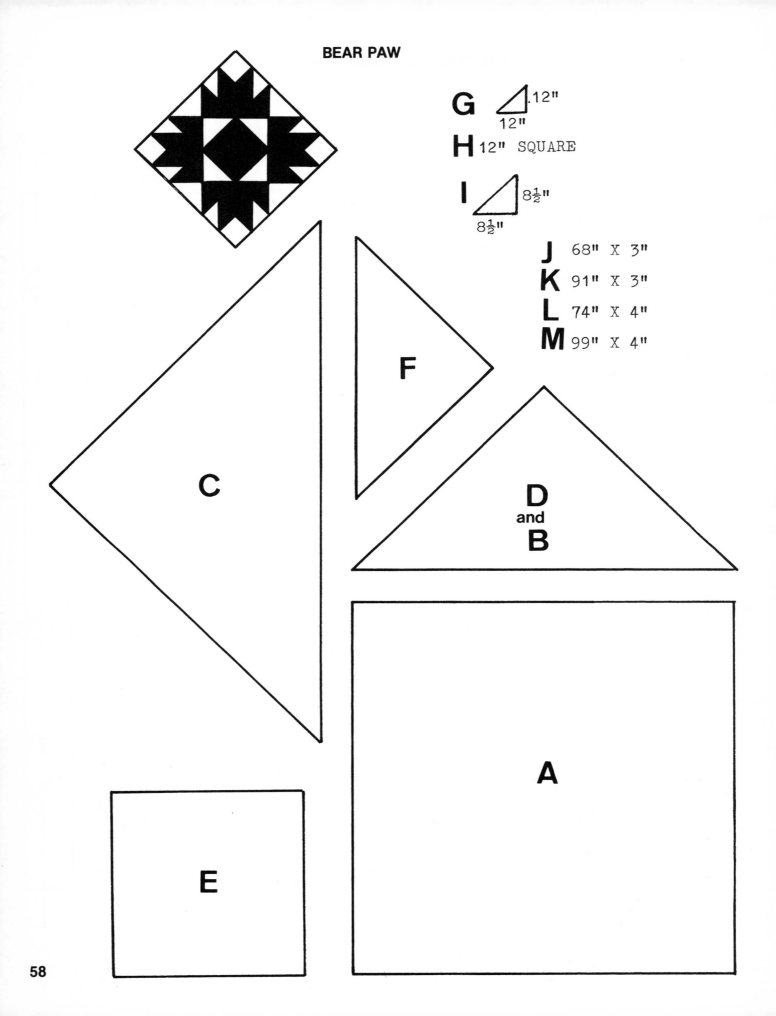

G ◿ .12"
  12"

H 12" SQUARE

I ◿ 8½"
  8½"

J 68" X 3"
K 91" X 3"
L 74" X 4"
M 99" X 4"

C

F

D and B

E

A

VARIABLE STAR — 68" X 68"
12" BLOCK

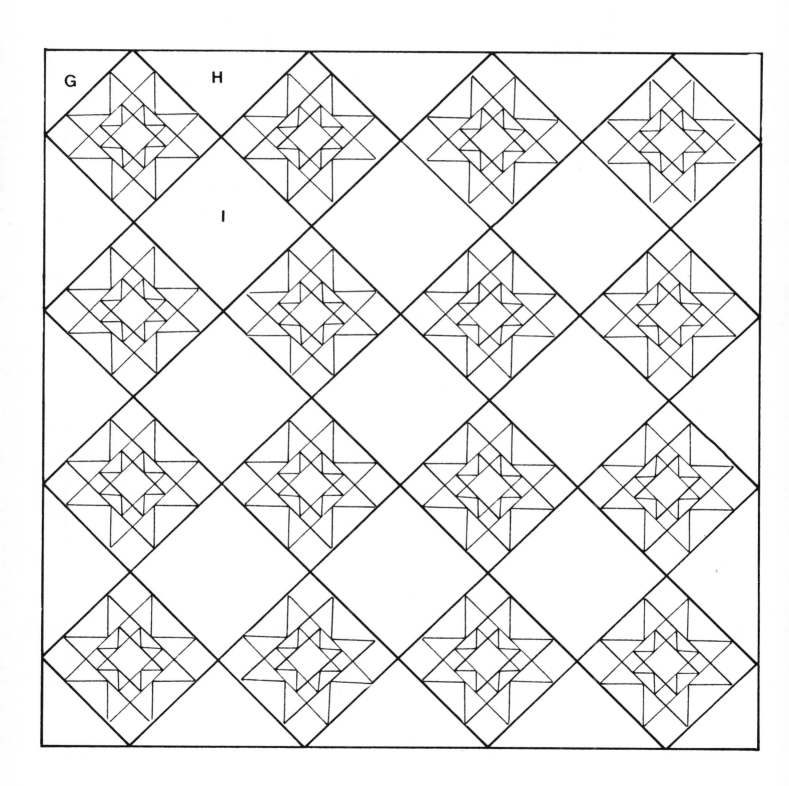

VARIABLE STAR

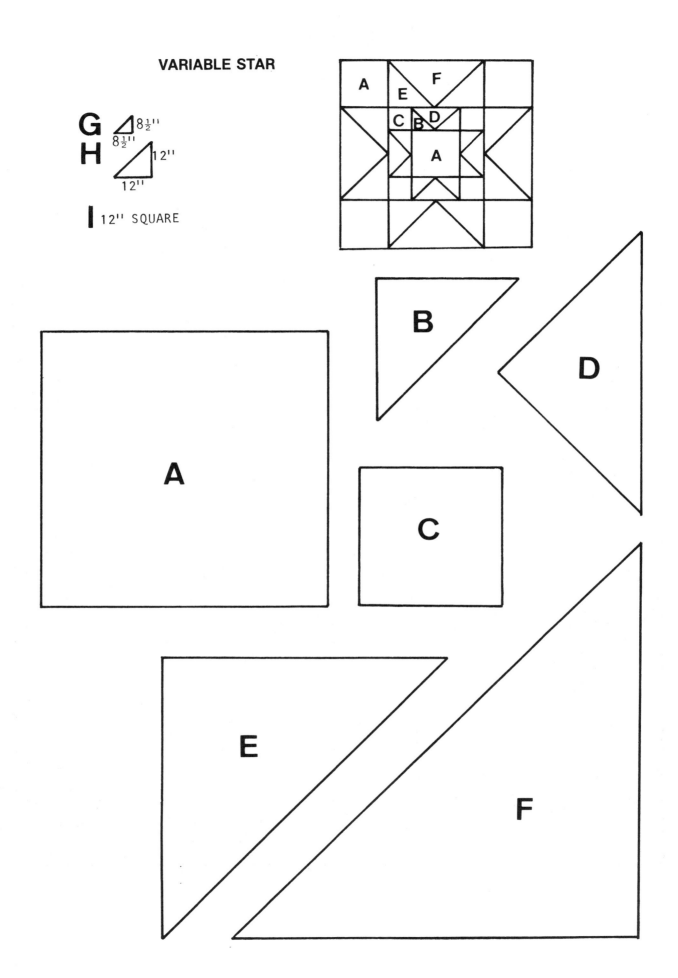

G △ 8½''
  8½''
H △ 12''
   12''

I | 12'' SQUARE

A

B

C

D

E

F

60

BASKETS — 75″ X 62¼″   9″ BLOCK

E

F

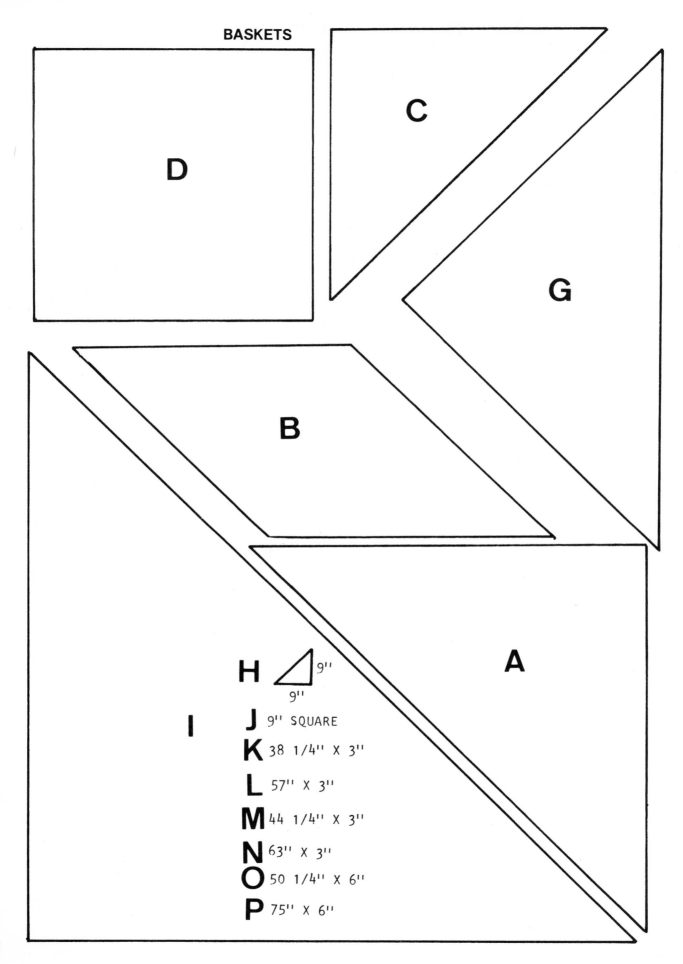

BASKETS

D

C

G

B

A

H   9''
    9''

I   J   9'' SQUARE

K   38 1/4'' X 3''

L   57'' X 3''

M   44 1/4'' X 3''

N   63'' X 3''

O   50 1/4'' X 6''

P   75'' X 6''

EIGHT POINTED STAR 1 — 79″ X 67″
12″ BLOCK

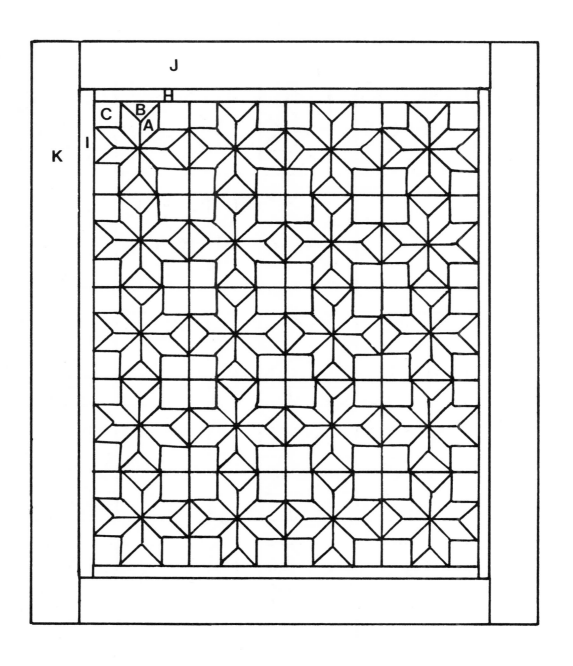

EIGHT POINTED STAR 2 — 92″ X 78″
12″ BLOCK

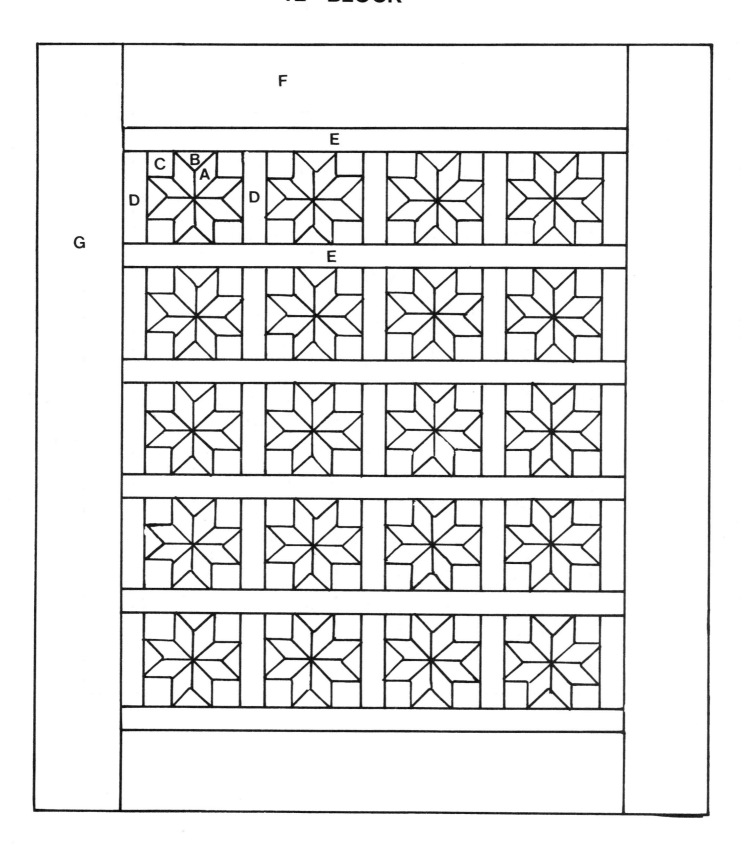

USE THESE TEMPLATES FOR BOTH 8 POINTED STAR QUILTS

D 12" X 2"

E 58" X 2"

F 58" X 10"

G 92" X 10"

H 48" X 1 1/2"

I 63" X 1 1/2"

J 51" X 8"

K 79" X 8"

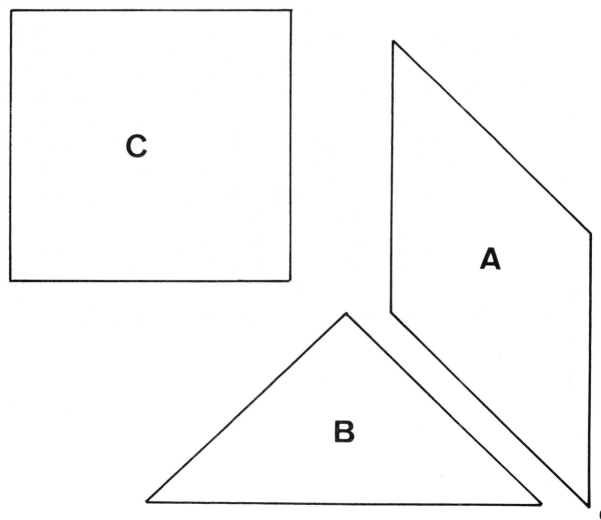

DOUBLE PINWHEEL — 75″ X 75″
10″ BLOCK

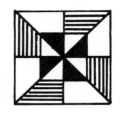

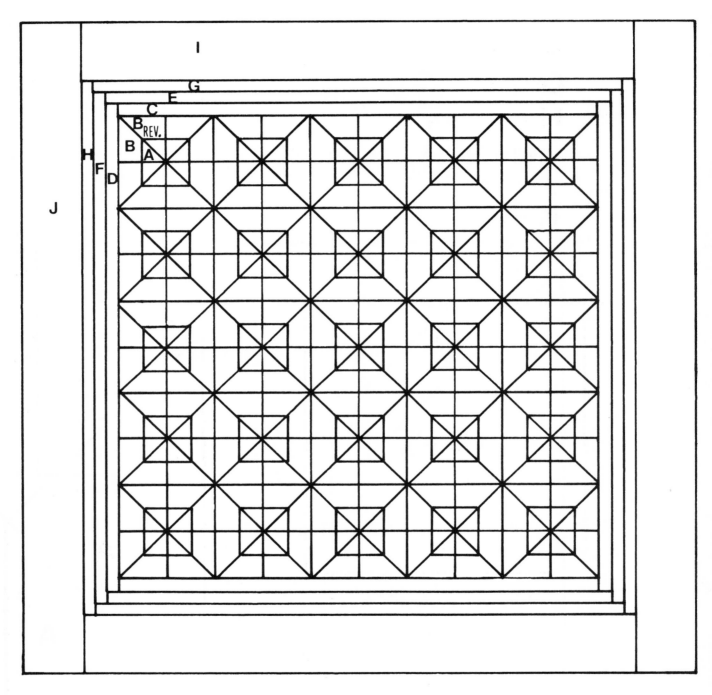

C 50'' X 1 1/2''

D 53'' X 1 1/2''

E 53'' X 1 1/2''

F 56'' X 1 1/2''

G 56'' X 1 1/2''

H 59'' X 1 1/2''

I 59'' X 8''

J 75'' X 8''

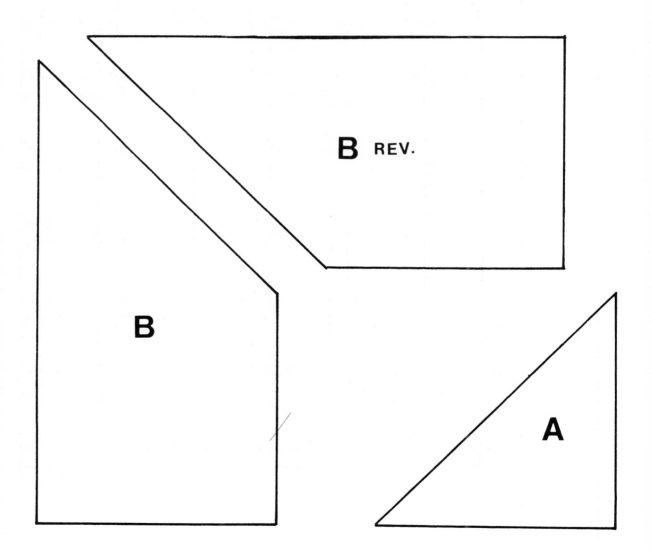

STARS AND STRIPES — 129″ X 103″

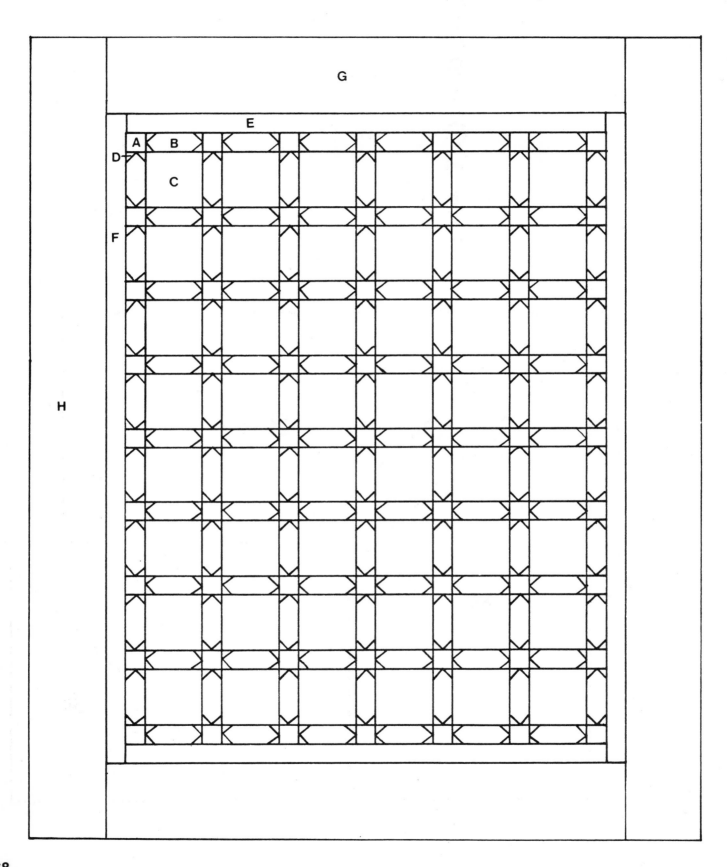

STARS AND STRIPES

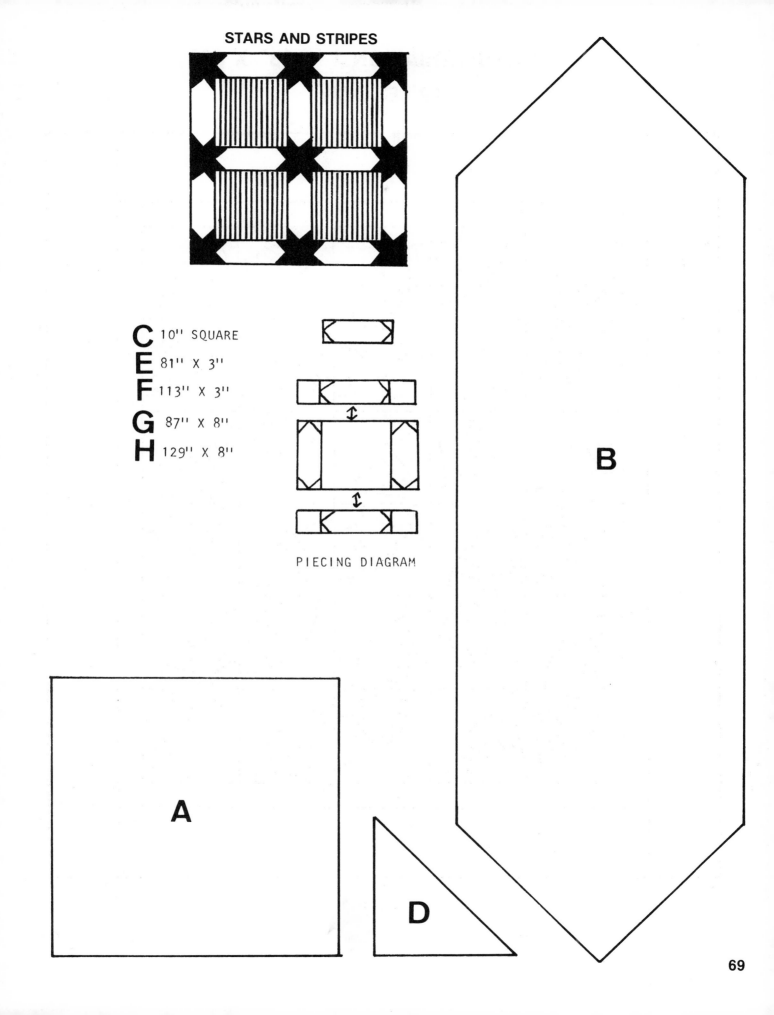

C 10" SQUARE

E 81" X 3"

F 113" X 3"

G 87" X 8"

H 129" X 8"

PIECING DIAGRAM

A

B

D

FANS VARIATION 1 — 98″ X 86″
12″ BLOCK

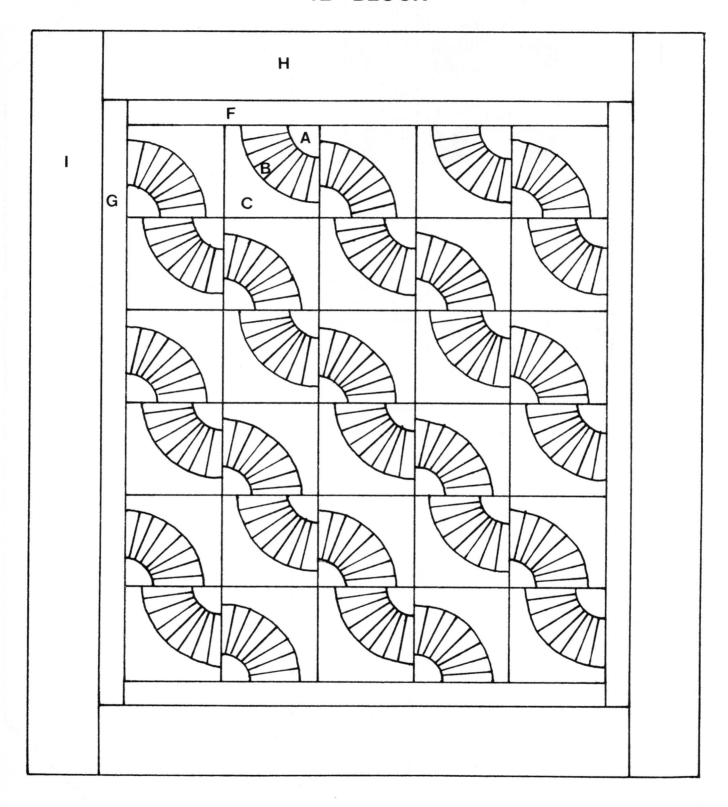

FANS VARIATION 2 — 72″ X 72″
12″ BLOCK

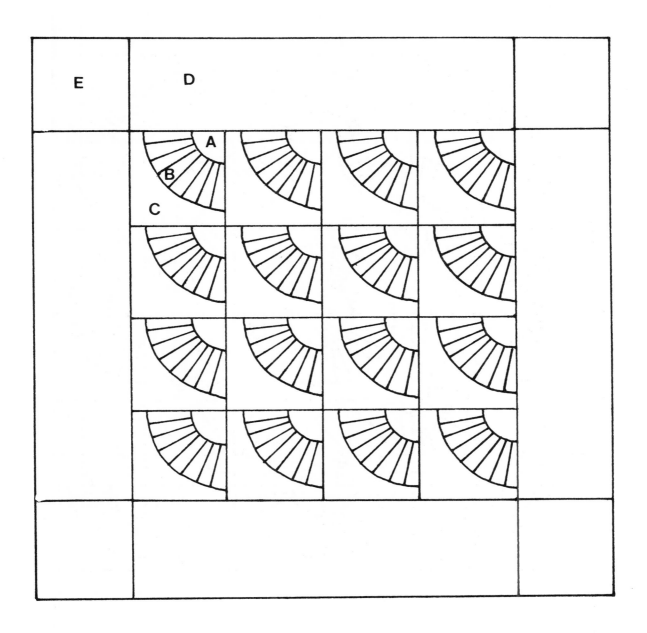

FANS VARIATION 3 — 92″ X 92″
12″ BLOCK

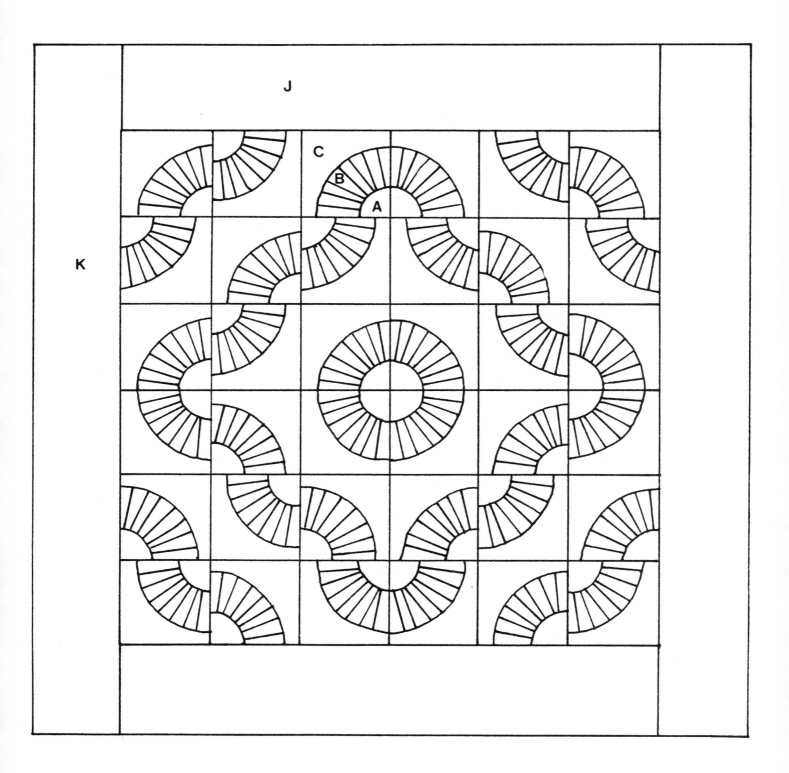

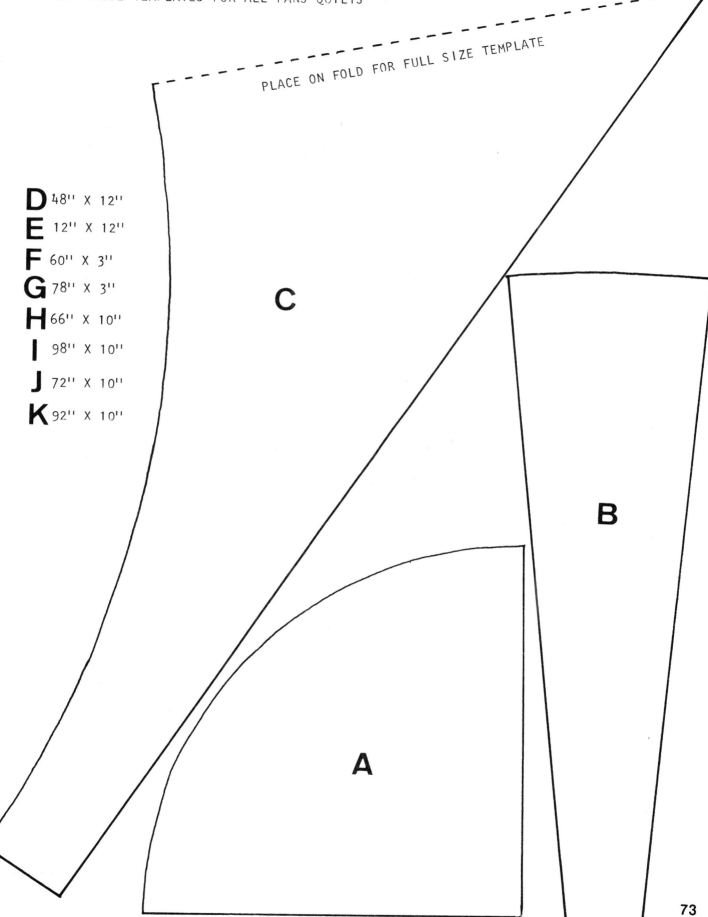

FANS

USE THESE TEMPLATES FOR ALL FANS QUILTS

PLACE ON FOLD FOR FULL SIZE TEMPLATE

D 48" X 12"
E 12" X 12"
F 60" X 3"
G 78" X 3"
H 66" X 10"
I 98" X 10"
J 72" X 10"
K 92" X 10"

C

B

A

HONEYCOMB — 56″ X 72″

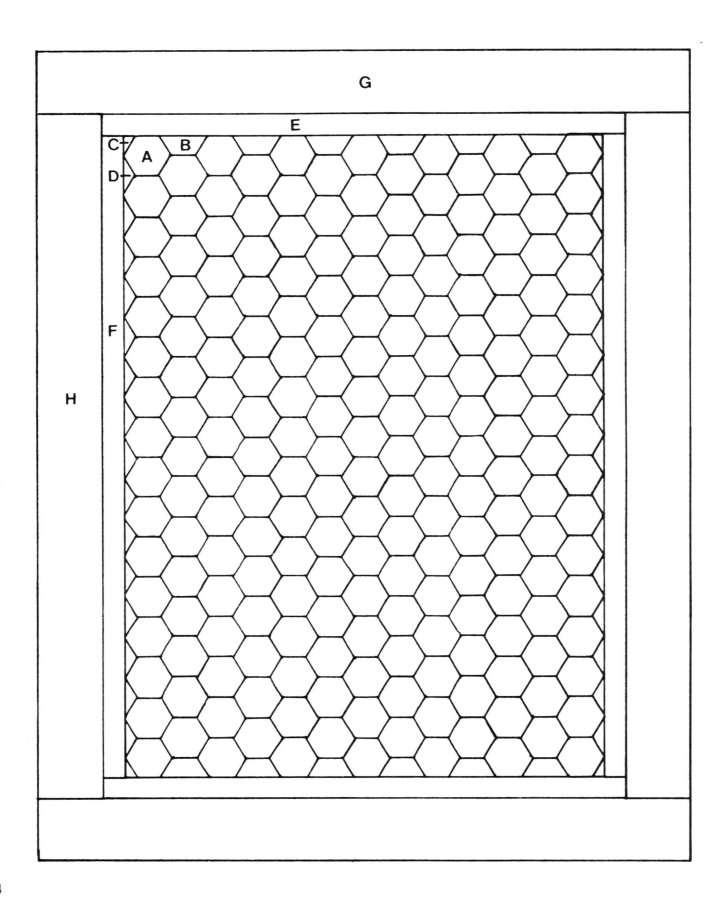

HONEYCOMB

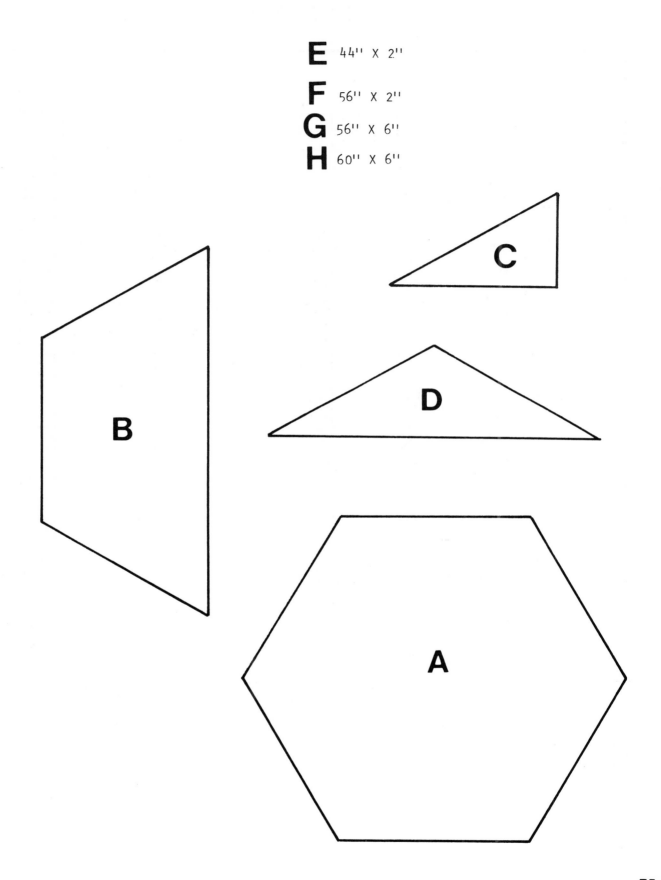

E 44'' X 2''

F 56'' X 2''

G 56'' X 6''

H 60'' X 6''

C

D

B

A

ROMAN STRIPES — 88″ X 78″
10″ BLOCK (SEE BACK COVER PHOTO)

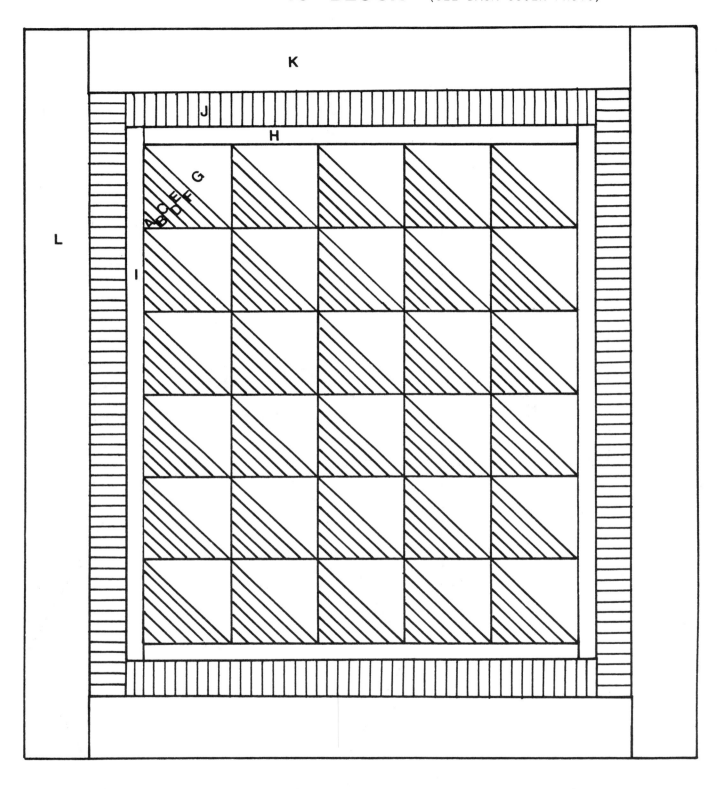

H 50″ X 2″	**K** 62″ X 8″
I 64″ X 2″	**L** 88″ X 8″

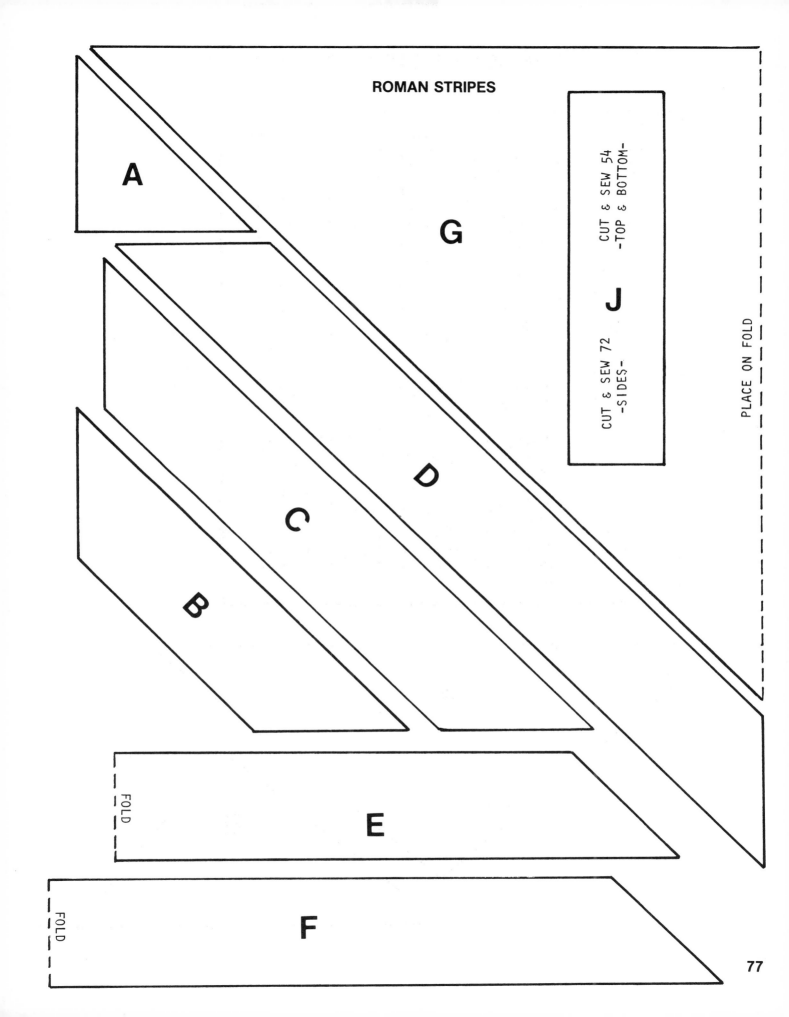

ROMAN STRIPES

A

G

J

CUT & SEW 54
—TOP & BOTTOM—

CUT & SEW 72
—SIDES—

PLACE ON FOLD

B

C

D

E

FOLD

F

FOLD

77

STREAK OF LIGHTNING — 66″ X 52″

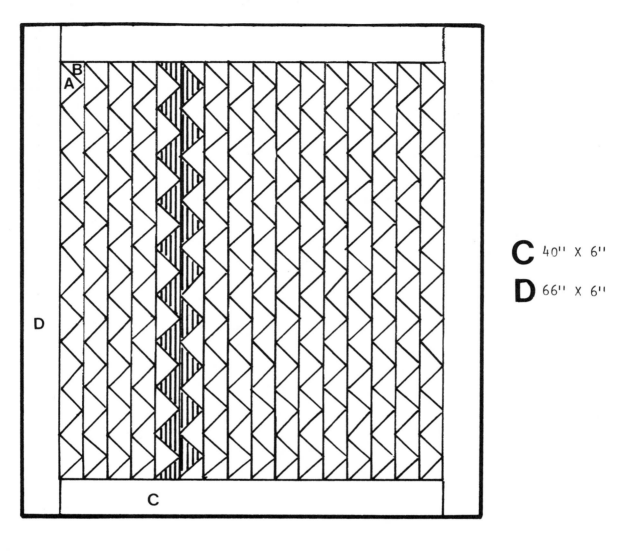

C 40″ X 6″

D 66″ X 6″

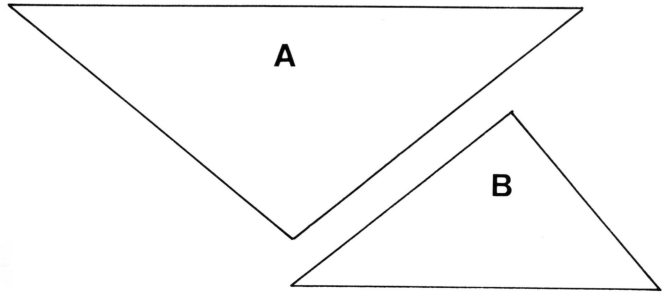

A

B

WILD GOOSE CHASE — 62" X 70"

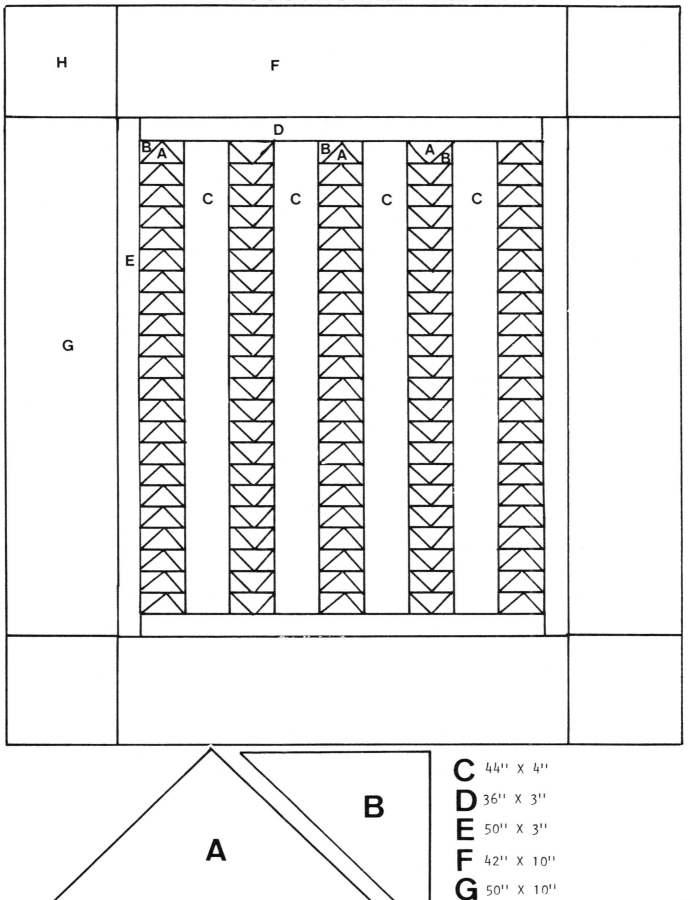

C 44" X 4"

D 36" X 3"

E 50" X 3"

F 42" X 10"

G 50" X 10"

H 10" SQUARE

STAR WITHIN A STAR — 58" X 60"

(SEE BACK COVER PHOTO)

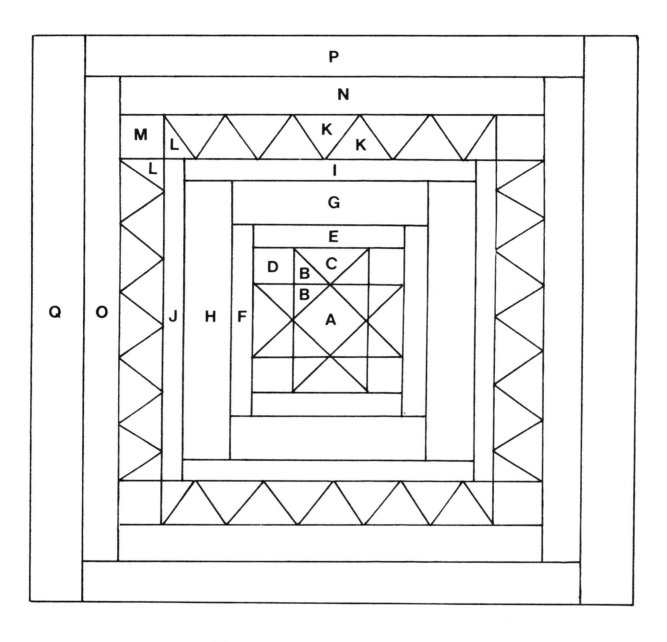

E 16" X 2 1/2"

F 21" X 2 1/2"

G 21" X 4 1/2"

H 30" X 4 1/2"

I 30" X 2 1/2"

J 35" X 2 1/2"

N 42" X 4"

O 50" X 4"

P 50" X 4"

Q 58" X 5"

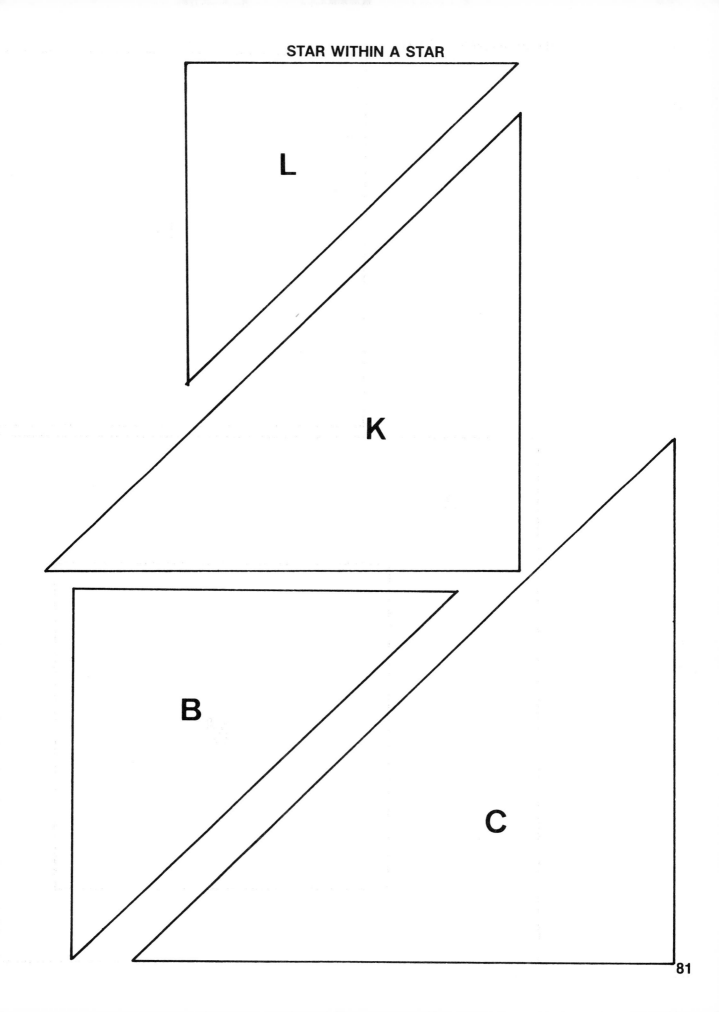

D

A

M

STAR WITHIN A STAR

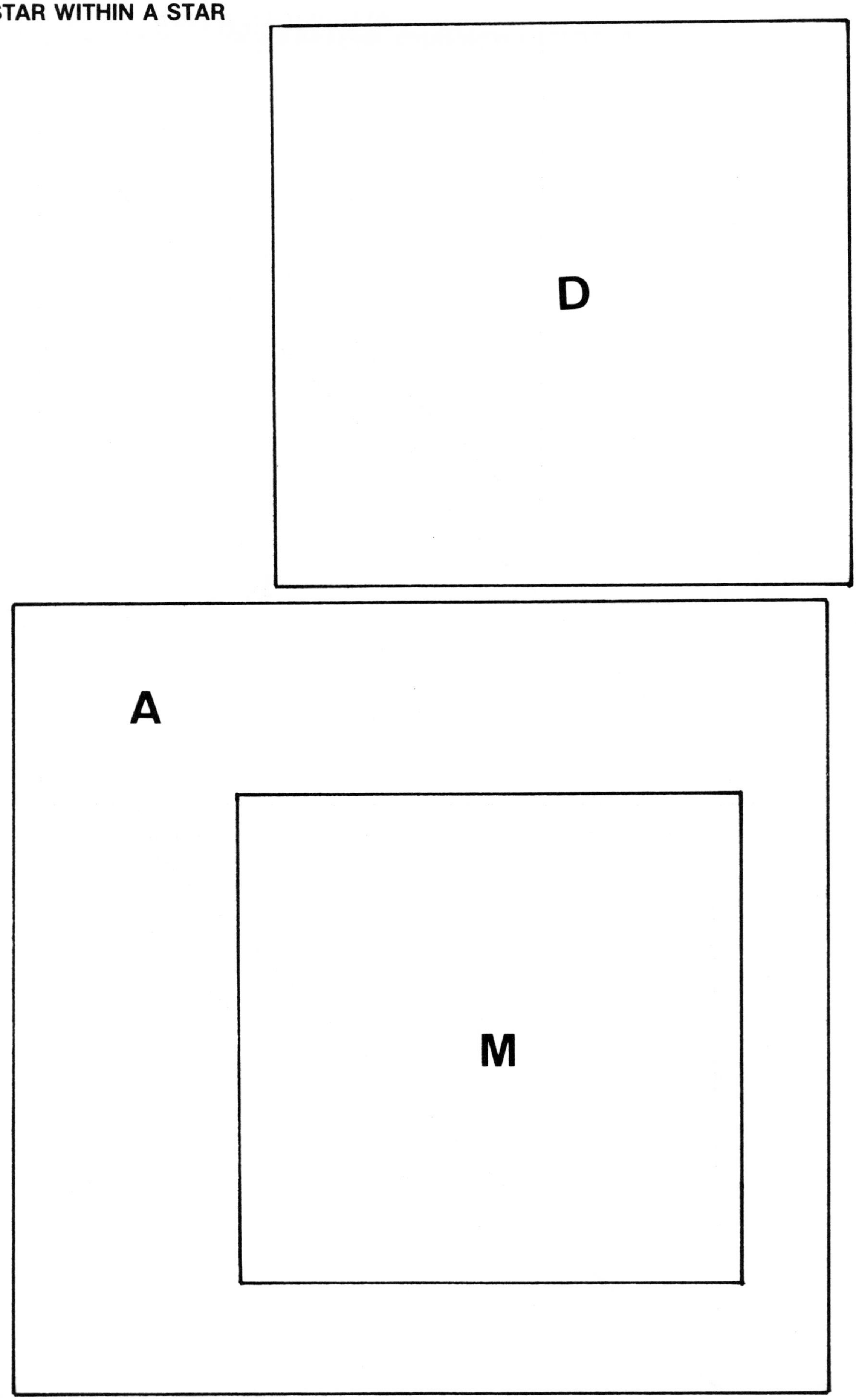

INTERLOCKING SQUARES — 24″ X 41″

(SEE FRONT COVER PHOTO)

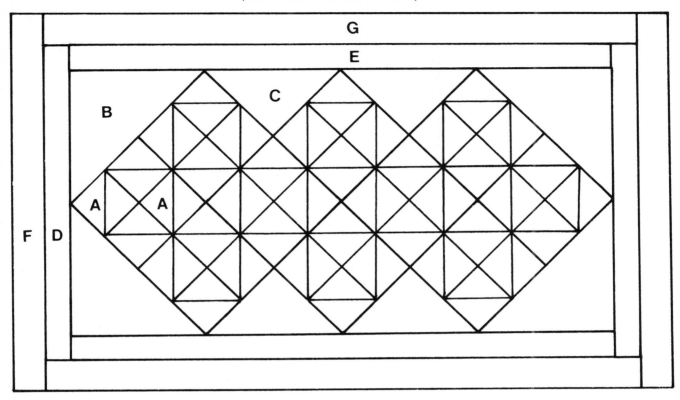

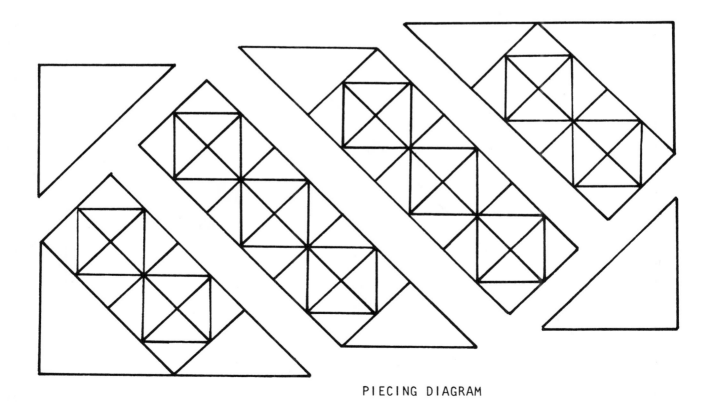

PIECING DIAGRAM

INTERLOCKING SQUARES

D 20 1/2'' X 1 3/4''

E 34'' X 1 3/4''

F 24'' X 1 3/4''

G 37 1/2'' X 1 3/4''

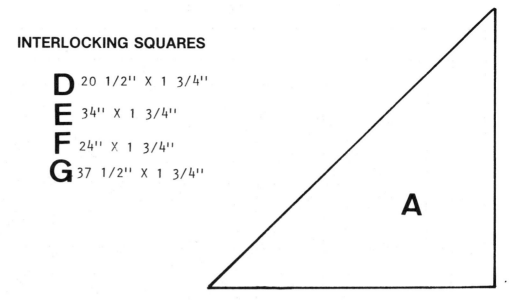

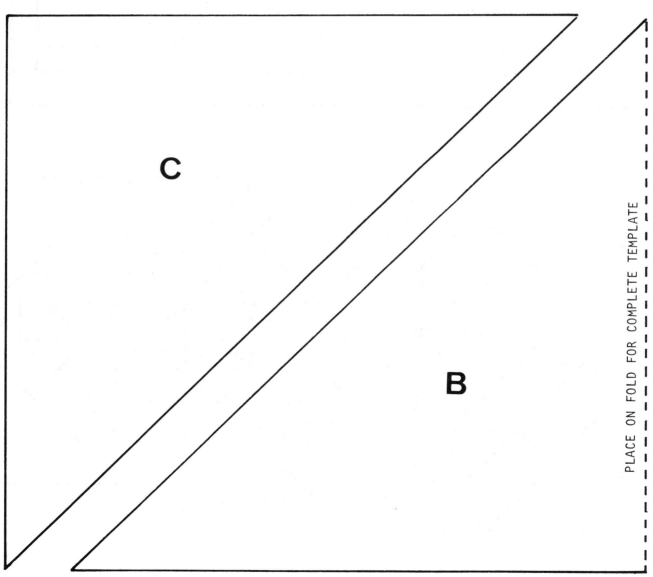

A

C

B

PLACE ON FOLD FOR COMPLETE TEMPLATE

OCEAN WAVES — 57" X 74"

THIS IS A GREAT QUILT FOR USING UP YOUR SCRAPS OF SOLIDS.
BLACK, USED AS THE BACKGROUND, REALLY SETS OFF THE "OCEAN WAVES".

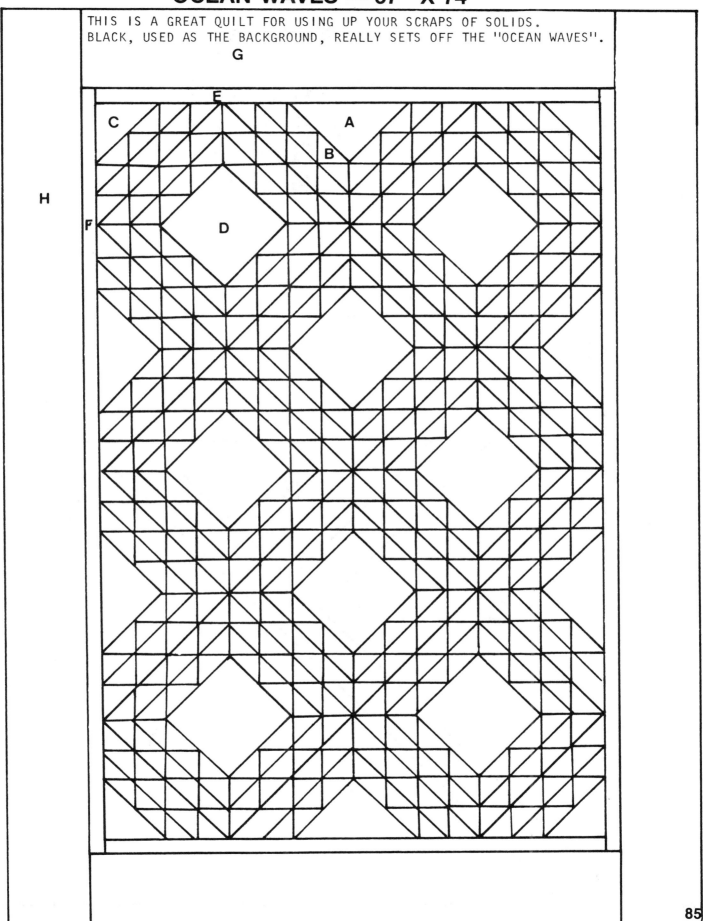

OCEAN WAVES

E 34" X 1 1/2"
F 54" X 1 1/2"
G 37" X 10"
H 74" X 10"

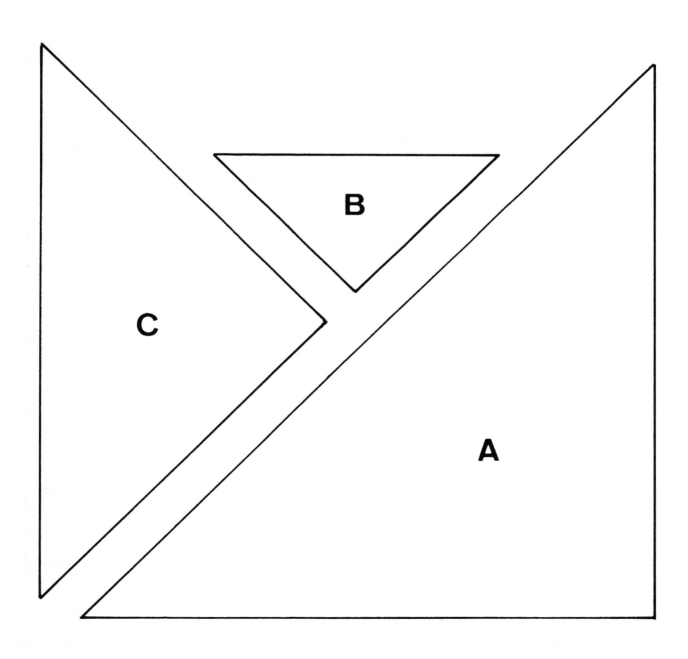

OCEAN WAVES

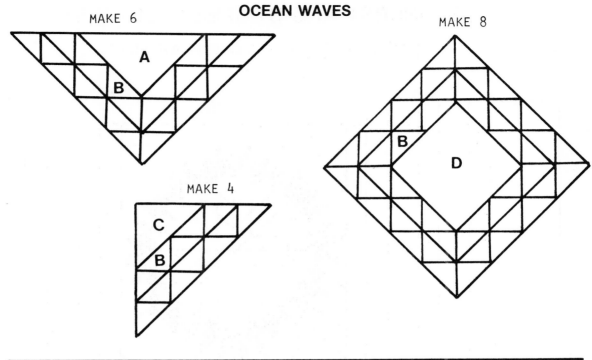

MAKE 6

A

B

MAKE 4

C

B

MAKE 8

B

D

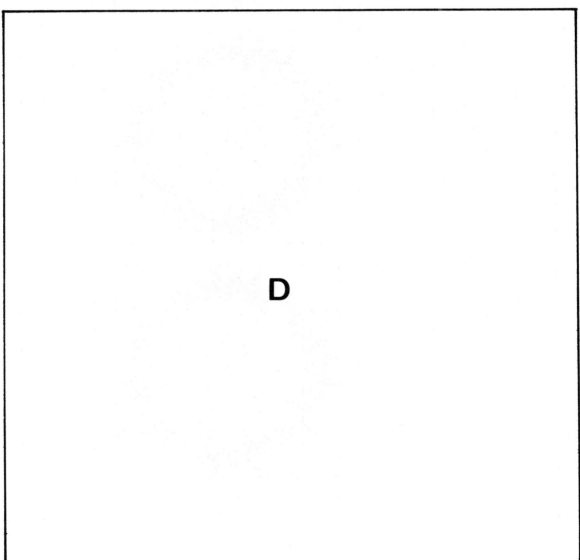

D

STARBURST AND STRIPES — 58″ X 61″
17″ BLOCK   (SEE FRONT COVER PHOTO)

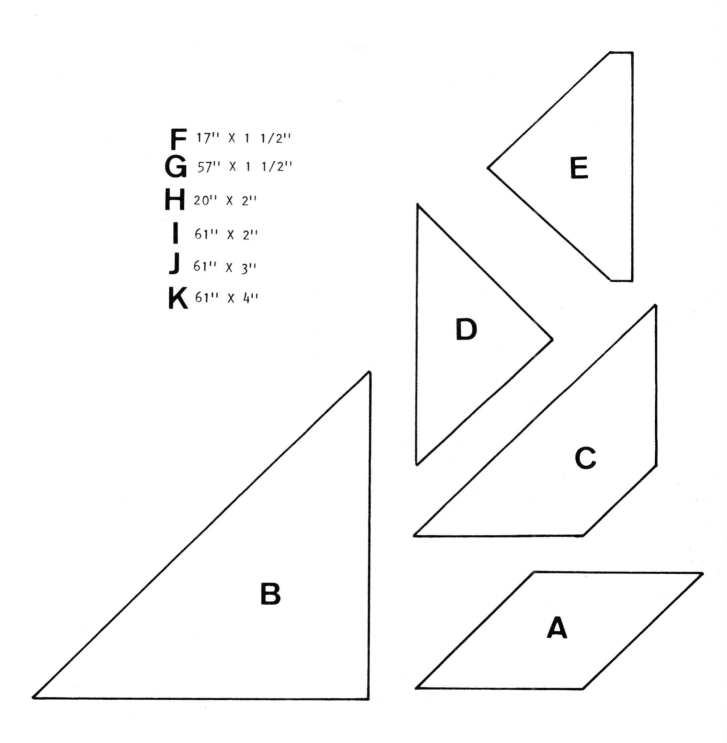

F 17" X 1 1/2"
G 57" X 1 1/2"
H 20" X 2"
I 61" X 2"
J 61" X 3"
K 61" X 4"

RAILROAD CROSSING — 80″ X 80″
18″ BLOCK

I MARKED THE PIECING LINES IN THE FIRST BLOCK ONLY, SHOWING M AND M REV.
IF YOU USE THE SAME COLOR FOR M AND M REV. AS YOU USE FOR C, E AND H IT
WILL GIVE THE STAR AND TRIANGLES A FLOATING EFFECT. THIS IS ANOTHER GOOD
QUILT FOR COLORFUL SCRAPS.

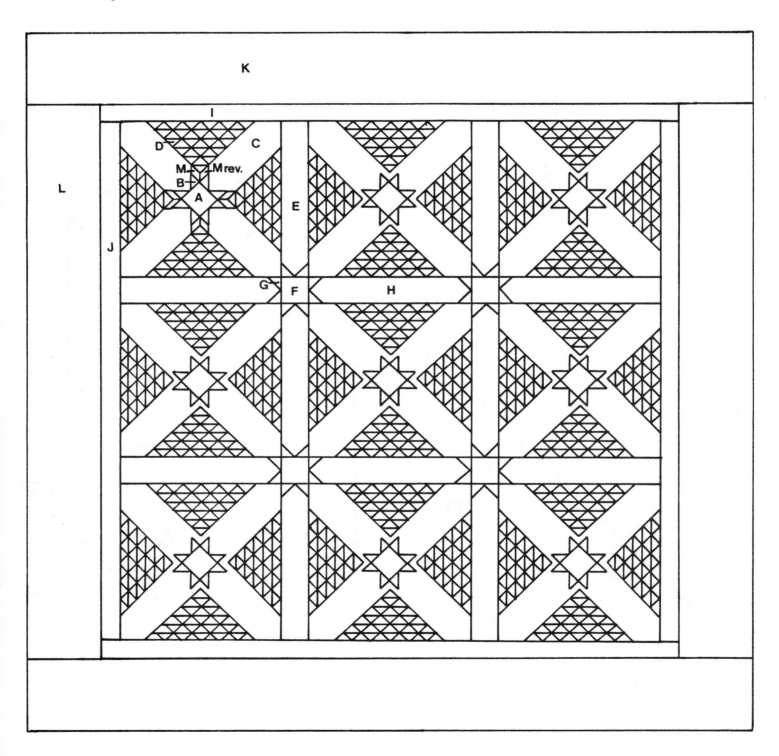

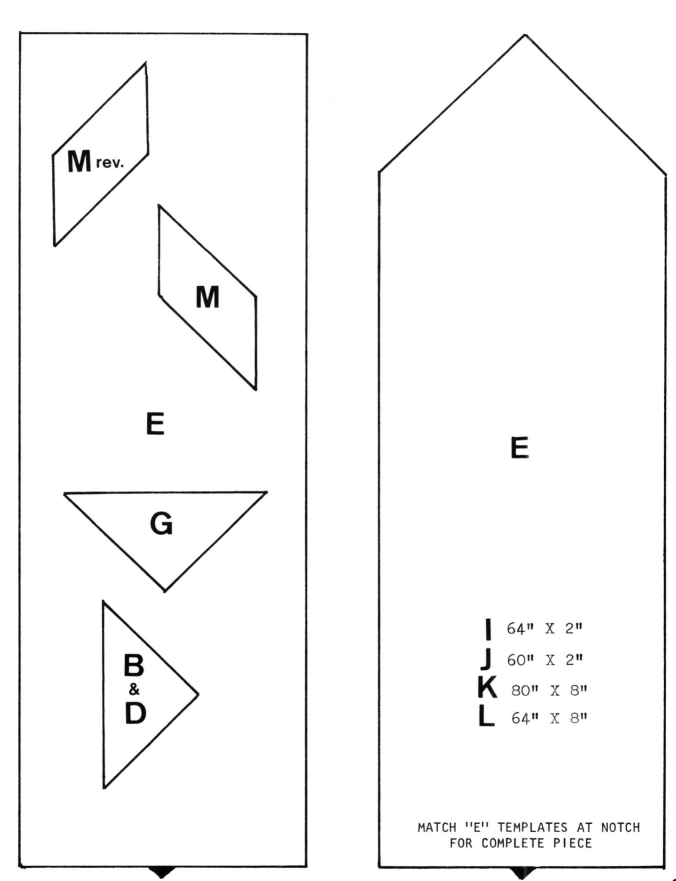

M rev.

M

E

G

B & D

E

I 64" X 2"
J 60" X 2"
K 80" X 8"
L 64" X 8"

MATCH "E" TEMPLATES AT NOTCH
FOR COMPLETE PIECE

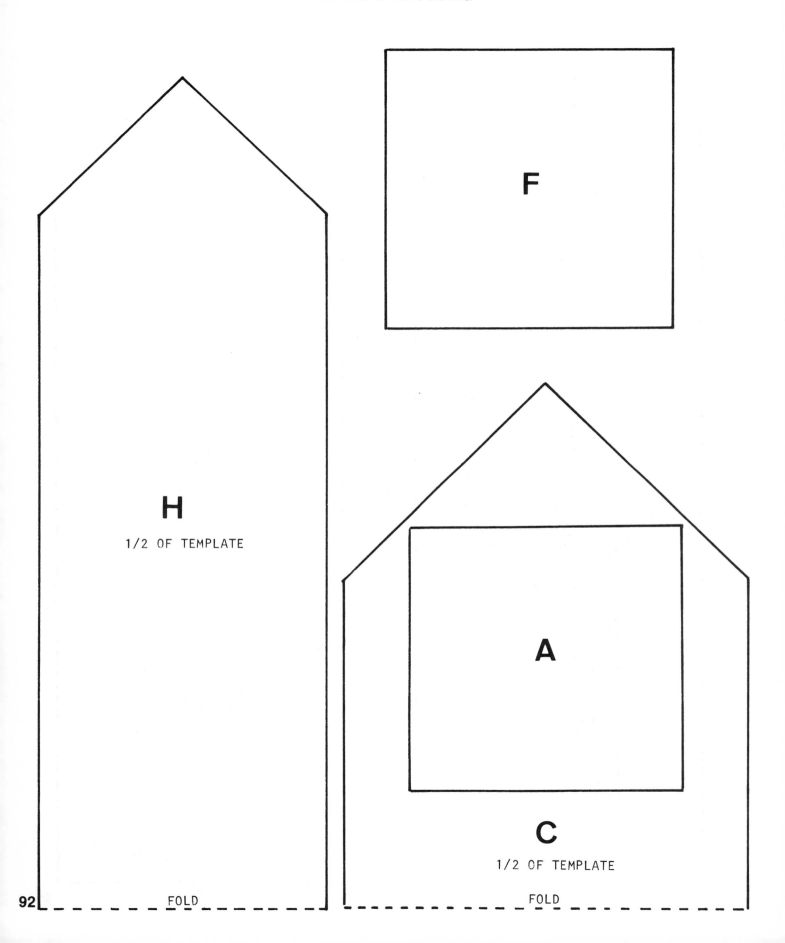

F

H

1/2 OF TEMPLATE

A

C

1/2 OF TEMPLATE

FOLD

FOLD

WINDMILL BLADES — 83" X 64"

18" BLOCK (see front cover photo)

WINDMILL BLADES

CONSEQUTIVE LETTERS REPRESENTING TEMPLATES
INCLUDE PREVIOUS PIECE OR PIECES.
EXAMPLE:

K M O

THIS BLOCK IS PIECED LOG CABIN
FASHION, FROM THE CENTER - OUT.

V 18" X 1"

W 58" X 1"

X 58" X 1"

Y 79" X 1"

Z 60" X 1"

a 62" X 1"

b 81" X 1"

c 83" X 1"

Q O M K I G E

P R N L J H F D

S T

U

B

C

A

CHAPTER FOUR
QUILTING

AMISH QUILTING, BOTH THE STITCHES THEMSELVES AS WELL AS THE
CAREFULLY PLANNED AND OFTEN ELABORATE MOTIFS, ARE AN INSPIRATION
TO ALL OF US DESIRING SOME AMOUNT OF EXPERTISE WITH A NEEDLE. THE
FLOWING AND INTRICATE ARRANGEMENTS OF MOTIFS SEEM IN STARK CONTRAST
TO THE SIMPLE GEOMETRICS OF THE PIECED TOP. THE QUILTING IS
SECONDARY TO THE COLOR AND PIECED DESIGN. SINCE IT IS NOT AS
VISIBLE YET SERVES A DEFINITE FUNCTION IN HOLDING THE QUILT
TOGETHER, THE AMISH QUILTER WAS ABLE TO CREATE AND DECORATE IN A
WAY THAT WAS DISCOURAGED WHILE DESIGNING AND PIECING THE QUILT.

THE AMISH ARE A LOVING AND SOCIAL COMMUNITY OF PEOPLE. WHETHER IT
BE PUTTING UP A BARN, HARVESTING, QUILTING AT A "BEE" OR ANY
OCCASIONS REQUIRING A NUMBER OF PEOPLE, THE AMISH COMMITMENT AND
DESIRE TO HELP AND SHARE WITH ONE ANOTHER IS A PRIMARY CONCERN.
QUILTING "BEES" PROVIDED THE WOMEN WITH TIME TO VISIT AND FELLOW-
SHIP WHILE KEEPING THEIR HANDS BUSY AND PRODUCTIVE.

THE QUILTING MOTIFS USED BY THE AMISH SEEM TO FALL INTO SEVERAL
CATAGORIES AND IT IS THE VARIATIONS OF THESE THEMES THAT MAKE UP
THE MANY PATTERNS AND COMBINATIONS ONE SEES WHEN VIEWING AMISH
QUILTS. UNLIKE THE NON-REPRESENTATIONAL SHAPES OF THEIR PIECED
DESIGNS, THE QUILTING MOTIFS OFTEN REPRESENTED FLOWERS, HEARTS,
BASKETS, FRUIT AND VINES TO NAME A FEW. I HAVE CHOSEN SOME OF THE
MOTIFS THAT APPEAR TO ME TO BE COMMONLY USED AND DRAFTED THEM FOR
YOU WITH SOME VARIATIONS AND POSSIBILITIES. BUT AGAIN, I ENCOURAGE
YOU TO USE THEM CREATIVELY AND EXPAND UPON OR CHANGE ANY OF THEM
TO SUIT YOUR OWN PURPOSE AND AREA TO BE QUILTED.

MAKING TEMPLATES
AND
TRANSFERRING DESIGNS TO FABRIC

AMISH QUILTING DESIGNS AND TEMPLATES WERE OFTEN PASSED DOWN WITHIN
FAMILIES AND COMMUNITIES. THESE GROUPS CONSISTED OF A FEW WOMEN WHO
HAD GAINED SUCH PROFICIENCY AT MARKING QUILTS THAT THEY WERE ABLE
TO DO IT FREEHAND WITHOUT THE AID OF TEMPLATES. ALTHOUGH I FIND
THIS ADMIRABLE, I ALWAYS PRE-DESIGN MY QUILTING AND THEN TRANSFER
IT TO MY COMPLETED TOP. I USE A VARIETY OF TECHNIQUES DEPENDING ON
THE MOTIFS I AM WORKING WITH. THERE ARE MANY WAYS TO MARK A TOP FOR
QUILTING AND THE IDEAS I AM PUTTING FORTH ARE THOSE THAT WORK BEST
FOR ME. IF YOU HAVE AN IDEA THAT WORKS BETTER OR YOU ARE MORE
COMFORTABLE WITH, THEN BY ALL MEANS USE IT. WHATEVER METHOD YOU
USE, IT IS ALWAYS WISE TO TEST IT FIRST TO MAKE SURE IT CAN BE
EASILY REMOVED FROM THE FABRIC YOU ARE USING.

MOST OF MY DESIGNS ARE INTRICATE AND NOT EASILY CUT INTO TEMPLATES.
(TEMPLATES BEING A FIRM SHAPE TO BE TRACED AROUND ONTO THE FABRIC
LEAVING YOU WITH AN OUTLINE OF THAT SHAPE.) I USE DRESSMAKERS CARBON
PAPER IN WHITE OR A LIGHT COLOR. ALONG WITH THE DRESSMAKERS CARBON

PAPER I USE A DRESSMAKERS TRACING WHEEL. WHEN USING A TRACING WHEEL MAKE SURE THE SURFACE YOU ARE TRACING OVER IS NOT EASILY MARRED. TRY USING A CARDBOARD CUTTING BOARD OR A LARGE DESK BLOTTER. FORMICA SURFACES DON'T ALLOW A DARK ENOUGH IMPRESSION TO BE MADE ON THE CLOTH AS THE TEETH OF THE WHEEL CAN'T PENETRATE THE DRESSMAKERS CARBON PAPER ON SUCH A HARD SURFACE.

NEXT, I PIN OR TAPE (MASKING TAPE ONLY, SCOTCH TAPE WILL LEAVE MARKS) MY QUILT TOP TO THE CUTTING BOARD OR OTHER SURFACE TO HOLD IT IN PLACE.

TRANSFER THE CHOSEN QUILTING MOTIFS TO TRACING OR TISSUE PAPER, MAKING SEVERAL COPIES IF IT IS TO BE USED OVER AND OVER. PLACE DRESSMAKERS CARBON PAPER OVER THE AREA TO BE MARKED AND PIN THE MOTIF ON TOP OF IT. CAREFULLY AND SLOWLY GUIDE THE TRACING WHEEL AROUND THE OUTLINES OF YOUR DESIGN. IN SOME CASES THE MOTIFS I USE ARE TOO INTRICATE FOR THE TRACING WHEEL. IT DOES NOT DO SMALL ROUNDED AREAS WELL. FOR THESE I USE THE ROUNDED HOOK END OF A SMALL CROCHET HOOK AND PRESS AROUND THE MOTIFS AS IF USING A PENCIL. I CAN BEAR DOWN ON IT AS NEEDED AND DO NOT HAVE TO WORRY ABOUT MARKING MY QUILT NEEDLESSLY WITH LEAD OR INK. ALWAYS TEST YOUR DRESSMAKERS CARBON PAPER ON A SWATCH OF THE FABRIC YOU ARE USING TO BE SURE IT WILL DISAPPEAR WITH A DAMP CLOTH OR STEAM IRON HELD <u>ABOVE</u> YOUR QUILT, NOT ON IT!

SOMETIMES DURING THE QUILTING MY MARKS BEGIN DISAPPEARING. I SIMPLY GO OVER THESE LIGHTLY WITH A WHITE OR LIGHT LEADED PENCIL.

MANY OTHER MOTIFS ARE SUITABLE SHAPES FOR MAKING PLASTIC OR CARDBOARD TEMPLATES. THESE WILL BE SHAPES THAT CAN BE EASILY TRACED AROUND. SOME TEMPLATES ONLY HAVE AN OUTER EDGE, LIKE A COOKIE CUTTER, AND SOME HAVE CUT OUT AREAS WITHIN THE SHAPE AS WELL. USE TRACING PAPER TO TRACE OVER THE SHAPE WANTED AND THEN GLUE IT TO STIFF CARDBOARD WITH RUBBER CEMENT. CUT AROUND TRACED SHAPE. TRANSPARENT PLASTIC WILL ELIMINATE THIS STEP AND WILL GIVE YOU A TEMPLATE THAT WILL LAST A LONG TIME.

I DO NOT USE TEMPLATES FOR FEATHERS, CABLES OR OTHER CONTINOUS QUILTING DESIGNS NOR DO I DESIGN DIRECTLY ONTO MY FABRIC. I CUT OR DRAW EXACT BORDER MEASUREMENTS FROM PAPER AND DO MY DESIGNING ON THAT. OFTEN, I NEED TO ADJUST OR CHANGE MY DESIGN TO FIT THE AREA TO BE QUILTED BETTER AND I WOULD RATHER DO IT ON PAPER THAN CHANCE MARKING MY FABRIC NEEDLESSLY. WHEN I AM SURE MY DESIGN IS COMPLETE AND FITS THE WAY I WANT IT TO, I USE MY DRESSMAKERS CARBON PAPER AND TRACING WHEEL TO TRANSFER IT ONTO MY QUILT TOP.

FIRST TRANSFER ON ANY MOTIFS AND THEN DETERMINE HOW YOU WANT YOUR BACKGROUND TO LOOK. IF THE BACKGROUND IS TO CONSIST OF STRAIGHT LINES, THERE ARE SEVERAL GOOD PROCEDURES. (THE COMBINED LINES AND MOTIFS CAN ALSO BE DONE ON PAPER AND TRANSFERRED ALL AT ONCE.)
    METHOD 1.   USE THIN MASKING TAPE PLACED ACROSS AREAS TO BE MARKED AND STITCH NEXT TO THE EDGE OF IT. IT COMES IN MANY WIDTHS AND DOES NOT LEAVE RESIDUE ON THE FABRIC. (IT IS STILL A GOOD IDEAS TO TEST IT) THIS METHOD WILL ASSURE YOU OF QUILTING STRAIGHT, EVEN LINES.
    METHOD 2.   USE A RULER OR YARDSTICK (THE TRANSPARENT GRIDED RULERS ARE BEST) AND MARK LINES EVENLY, DIRECTLY ONTO YOUR FABRIC. I GENERALLY USE THIS METHOD AND ALWAYS MARK MY LINES AS LIGHTLY AS POSSIBLE.

QUILTING WITHIN THE PIECED DESIGN

THE CORNER SQUARES IN AMISH QUILTS WERE MANY TIMES IGNORED AS A SEPARATE PART OF THE PIECED DESIGN AND A FEATHER SCROLL OR CABLE MIGHT CONTINUE RIGHT OVER THE SEAMS TO THE END OF THE BORDER. THE CABLES, FEATHER SCROLLS OR OTHER DESIGNS WOULD SIMPLY STOP WHERE THE BORDER STOPPED. THE NEXT SIDE WOULD START AT THE TOP EDGE OF THIS QUILTING. THERE WAS NOT ANY OVERLAPPING, BUT IN MANY INSTANCES IT APPEARS NO PRECAUTIONS WERE TAKEN TO MAKE SURE ALL THE CORNERS WOULD BE THE SAME OR THAT THE DESIGN ITSELF WOULD BE UN-INTERRUPTED. ON A DIFFERENT PIECE THE QUILTING DESIGN MIGHT BE INTERRUPTED BY A CORNER SQUARE. THIS SQUARE WOULD THEN BE FILLED WITH A FEATHER WREATH, BASKET OR OTHER DESIGN. INNER BORDERS SEEM RARELY TO HAVE CONTINUOUS QUILTING AND THE CORNER SQUARES OF THESE OFTEN HAVE A SMALL FLORAL OR OTHER MOTIF SEEMINGLY UNRELATED TO THE REST OF THE BORDER. AMISH QUILTS, WITH THEIR MANY BORDERS, ARE OFTEN A VERITABLE SAMPLER OF QUILTING VARIATIONS.

CROSS HATCHING (CREATING MANY SMALL DIAMONDS OR SQUARES BY CROSSING A SERIES OF STRAIGHT LINES EQUAL DISTANCES APART) WAS COMMONLY USED FOR FILLING THE SURFACE OF A QUILT, EITHER ALL OR IN PART, DISREGARDING SEAM LINES. THIS IS VERY EFFECTIVE VISUALLY. ALTHOUGH THIS ALL-OVER CROSS HATCHING IS SOMETIMES THE CASE IN BARS QUILTS, THE CENTER BARS CAN ALSO BE FOUND QUILTED INDIVIDUALLY WITH CABLE, FEATHERS OR UNIQUE GEOMETRIC DESIGNS RUNNING THE LENGTH OF THE BAR.

CENTER DIAMONDS AND SQUARES OFFERED THE QUILTER LARGER AREAS FOR DESIGNING BIGGER AND MORE COMPLEX DESIGNS. LARGE EIGHT POINTED STAR MOTIFS, FEATHER WREATHS AND COMBINATIONS OF THESE WITH EXTENSIVE BACKGROUND QUILTING WERE COMMON.

THE TRIANGULAR AREAS SURROUNDING THE DIAMOND OR SQUARE WERE OFTEN FILLED WITH CROSS HATCHING OR OTHER BACKGROUND QUILTING AND ON SOME QUILTS YOU WILL FIND THIS AREA STITCHED WITH AN ORIGINAL FLORAL DESIGN, GRAPES AND VINES OR FEATHER VARIATIONS.

THERE ARE A FEW RULES I OBSERVE FOR OBTAINING A SUCCESSFUL QUILTING DESIGN.

ANY LINES QUILTED CLOSER TOGETHER THAN 1/2 INCH WILL GIVE VERY LITTLE, IF ANY, "POOF" OR TEXTURE. THE AREA QUILTED WILL SIMPLY RECEDE. THIS IS FINE IF IT IS THE EFFECT YOU WANT, BUT NOT DESIRABLE FOR CROSS HATCHING OR STRAIGHT LINE QUILTING WHERE TEXTURE IS TO BE THE OBJECTIVE.

WHEN I AM USING A PARTICULAR MOTIF THAT I WANT TO STAND OUT WITHIN A LARGE AREA, I USE A DIFFERENT SCALE FOR MY BACKGROUND THAN THAT OF THE MOTIF. SCALING THE BACKGROUND TO BE SMALLER WORKS BEST. THIS PROVIDES CONTRAST AND ALLOWS THE EYE TO SEPARATE THE QUILTING DESIGNS. IF THE MOTIF IS CURVED I USE STRAIGHT LINES FOR THE BACKGROUND. LIKEWISE, IF THE MOTIF CONSISTS OF STRAIGHT LINES THEN THE BACKGROUND SHOULD EITHER BE CURVED OR QUILTED WITH LINES THAT ARE AT A DIFFERENT ANGLE THAN THE MOTIF. AGAIN, IT IS THIS CONTRAST THAT ALLOWS THE EYE TO SEPARATE THE DESIGNS.

EXPERIMENT ON PAPER. A DRAWING TO SCALE WILL REVEAL THE NEED FOR MORE CONTRAST. WHAT YOU QUILT RECEDES AND WHAT YOU LEAVE UN-QUILTED WILL STAND OUT.

QUILTING THREAD

THE AMISH OFTEN USED BLACK QUILTING THREAD FOR THEIR QUILTING. I USE
BLACK THREAD ON ALMOST ALL OF MY QUILTS AS I LIKE THE WAY IT LOOKS.
IF THIS IS NEW TO YOU, YOU MIGHT WANT TO GIVE IT A TRY. EXPERIMENT
WITH SOME OTHER COLORS TOO. YOU MAY DECIDE YOU LIKE THE EFFECT.

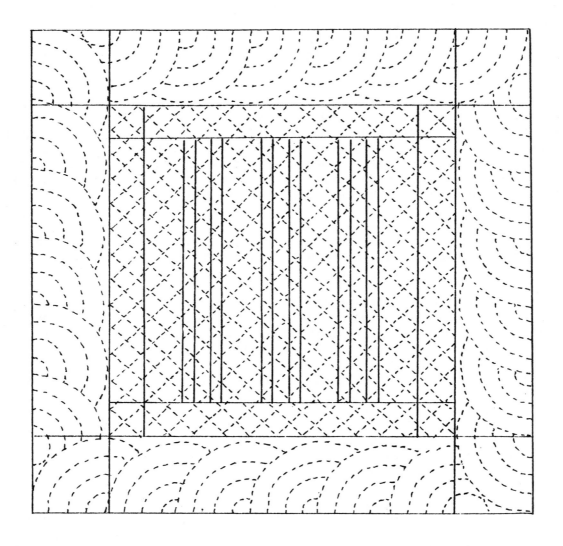

STRAIGHT LINE DESIGNS —
FOR BACKGROUNDS & BORDERS

CHANNELING OR STRAIGHT LINE

USE BOTH OF THESE LINE DESIGNS EITHER STRAIGHT OR ANGLED FOR BACKGROUNDS AND BORDERS. THE LINES ARE USUALLY A "THUMB" OR 3/4 INCH APART.

RODDING OR DOUBLING
(SETS OF DOUBLE LINES)

CROSS HATCHING FORMING SQUARES

CROSS HATCHING LINES ARE GENERALLY 1/2 INCH TO 1 INCH APART

CROSS HATCHING FORMING DIAMONDS

MARK DOTS AN EQUAL DISTANCE APART— ACROSS FROM ONE ANOTHER

CROSS HATCHING FOR NARROW BORDERS

CONNECT EVERY OTHER DOT.

GO BACK AND CONNECT EVERY OTHER DOT AGAIN USING ALTERNATE DOTS AND CROSSING LINES.

SOME STRAIGHT LINE DESIGNS FOR BORDERS.

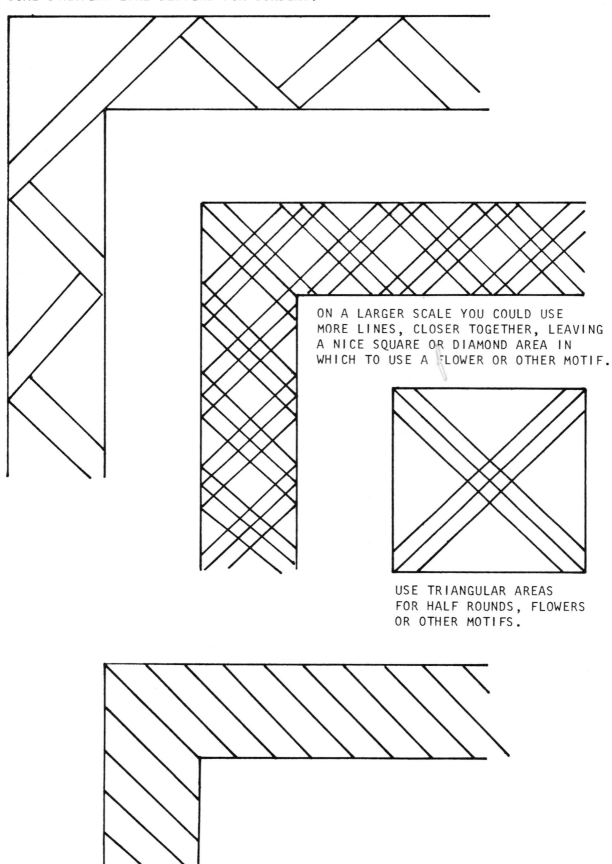

ON A LARGER SCALE YOU COULD USE
MORE LINES, CLOSER TOGETHER, LEAVING
A NICE SQUARE OR DIAMOND AREA IN
WHICH TO USE A FLOWER OR OTHER MOTIF.

USE TRIANGULAR AREAS
FOR HALF ROUNDS, FLOWERS
OR OTHER MOTIFS.

CIRCLE AND HALF CIRCLE DESIGNS

USE YOUR OWN COMPASS TO GET
LARGER CIRCLE TEMPLATES.

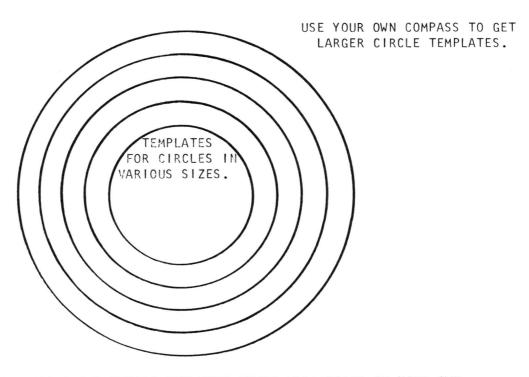

TEMPLATES
FOR CIRCLES IN
VARIOUS SIZES.

TRY THIS BORDER DESIGN AND EXPERIMENT WITH OTHER VARIATIONS OF YOUR OWN.

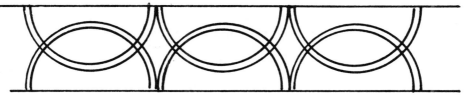

MARK HALF CIRCLES ON ONE SIDE OF BORDER.

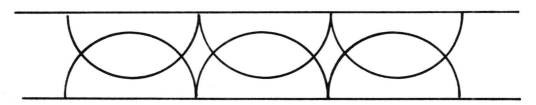

ADD HALF CIRCLES TO THE OTHER SIDE. DEPENDING ON YOUR SPACING, MANY
INTERESTING EFFECTS CAN BE PRODUCED. DOUBLE THE LINES, AS BELOW FOR YET ANOTHER
VARIATION.

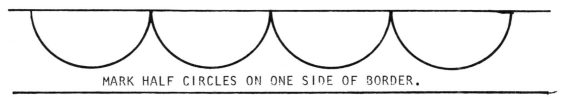

INTERLOCKING CIRCLES - TRACE AROUND CIRCLE TEMPLATE WITH CIRCLE EDGES
TOUCHING OR CLOSE.

GO BACK AND CENTER THIS ROW OF CIRCLES OVER TOUCHING SIDES OF PREVIOUS CIRCLES.

TRIANGLES PROVIDE GOOD AREAS
FOR HALF ROUNDS. THE END OF
YOUR SPOOL OF THREAD MAKES
A HANDY TEMPLATE.

USE A SERIES OF FOUR OR MORE HALF CIRCLES IN GRADUATING SIZES
TO PRODUCE THIS NEXT BORDER DESIGN.

PLACE HALF CIRCLES
SO THEY OVERLAP ACROSS
LENGTH OF BORDER. DO
NOT MARK AREAS WHERE
THEY OVERLAP.

USING NEXT SIZE SMALLER HALF ROUND TEMPLATE, REPEAT AS ABOVE.

CONTINUE ON UNTIL YOU REACH THE DESIRED EFFECT. CHANGING THE POINT
WHERE THEY OVERLAP WILL CHANGE THE DESIGN. EXPERIMENT WITH DIFFERENT SIZES.

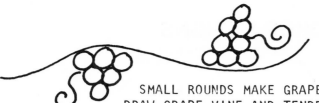

SMALL ROUNDS MAKE GRAPE CLUSTERS.
DRAW GRAPE VINE AND TENDRILS FREEHAND.

HALF ROUNDS WILL SCALLUP ANY EDGE.
USE THEM AROUND A CIRCLE OR ACROSS
A SEAM LINE TO FRAME OTHER MOTIFS.

HALF ROUNDS PARTIALLY FILL IN A SQUARE AND
SET A SMALL MOTIF OFF NICELY.

HALF ROUNDS COMBINED WITH STRAIGHT LINES PROVIDE GOOD TEXTURE.

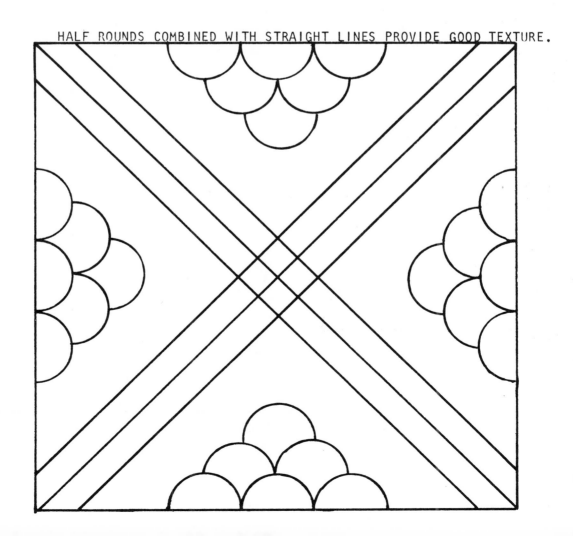

TEARDROP DESIGNS

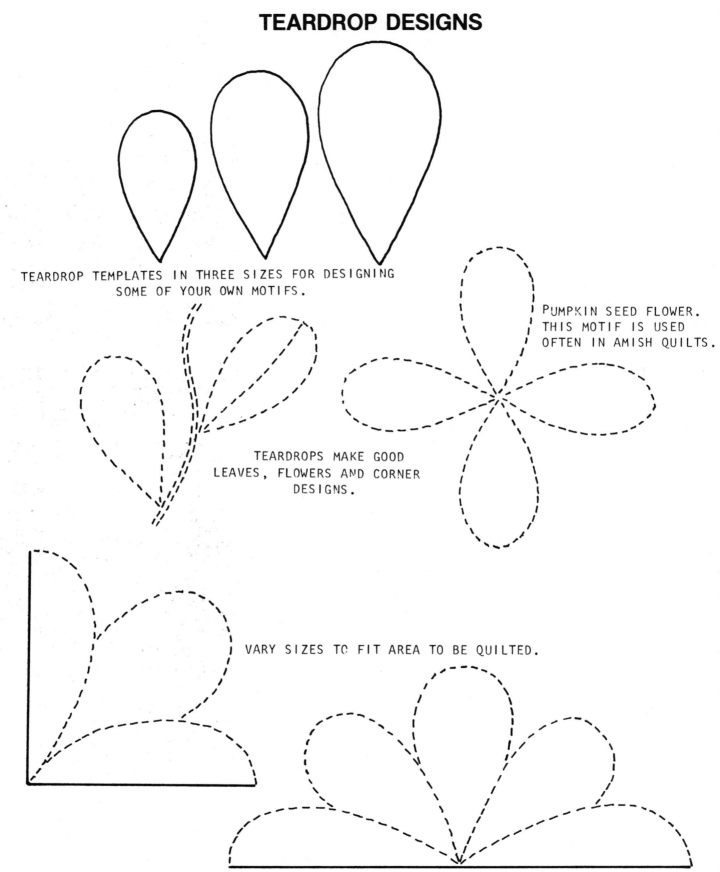

TEARDROP TEMPLATES IN THREE SIZES FOR DESIGNING SOME OF YOUR OWN MOTIFS.

PUMPKIN SEED FLOWER. THIS MOTIF IS USED OFTEN IN AMISH QUILTS.

TEARDROPS MAKE GOOD LEAVES, FLOWERS AND CORNER DESIGNS.

VARY SIZES TO FIT AREA TO BE QUILTED.

THIS TYPE OF MOTIF IS GOOD TO USE IN AREAS LEFT BY SOME STRAIGHT LINE DESIGNS.

FEATHER DESIGNS

FEATHER DESIGNS OFTEN CONSIST OF A "SPINE" (THE LINE THE FEATHERS FOLLOW) AND A FEATHER TEMPLATE. THE SPINE WILL DICTATE THE MOVEMENT AND SHAPE OF YOUR DESIGN. IT CAN BE DOUBLE OR SINGLE.

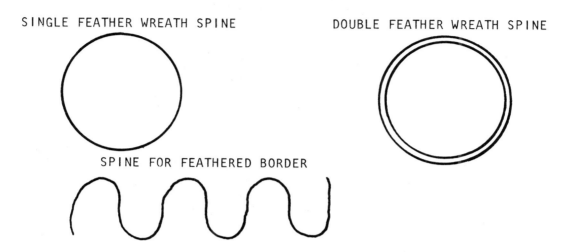

SINGLE FEATHER WREATH SPINE   DOUBLE FEATHER WREATH SPINE

SPINE FOR FEATHERED BORDER

THE SPINE CAN BE STRAIGHT, CURVED OR TAKE ON ANY SHAPE YOU WANT TO USE. FEATHERS USUALLY FOLLOW ALONG BOTH SIDES OF THE SPINE. THE SIZE OF THE FEATHER TEMPLATE YOU USE WILL DEPEND ON THE SIZE OF THE AREA TO BE QUILTED.

FEATHER TEMPLATES IN 4 SIZES AND SHAPES

WHEN DRAWING YOUR SPINE REMEMBER TO LEAVE ROOM FOR FEATHERS ON TOP AND BOTTOM. WHEN DRAWING A SPINE FOR FEATHER WREATHS, DRAW GUIDE LINES ON BOTH SIDES TO MAINTAIN AN EVEN DESIGN ALL AROUND.

FEATHERS HAVE THE LOOK OF ONE OVERLAPPING THE OTHER. WHEN DRAWING THEM
YOU WILL HAVE LINES THAT CAN BE ELIMINATED LATER FOR YOUR FINAL CLEAN DRAFT.
(SEE BROKEN LINES IN ILLUSTRATION)

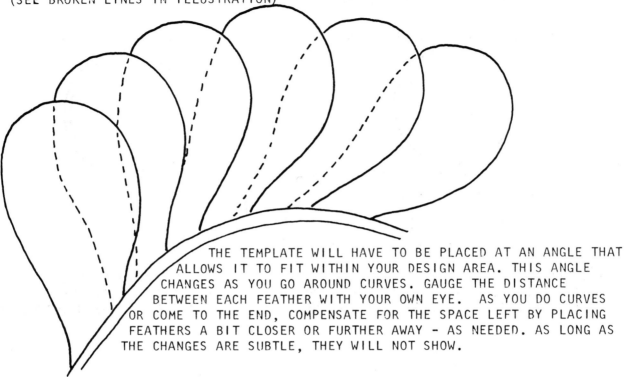

THE TEMPLATE WILL HAVE TO BE PLACED AT AN ANGLE THAT
ALLOWS IT TO FIT WITHIN YOUR DESIGN AREA. THIS ANGLE
CHANGES AS YOU GO AROUND CURVES. GAUGE THE DISTANCE
BETWEEN EACH FEATHER WITH YOUR OWN EYE. AS YOU DO CURVES
OR COME TO THE END, COMPENSATE FOR THE SPACE LEFT BY PLACING
FEATHERS A BIT CLOSER OR FURTHER AWAY - AS NEEDED. AS LONG AS
THE CHANGES ARE SUBTLE, THEY WILL NOT SHOW.

WHEN DRAWING THE OPPOSITE SIDE OF A FEATHER DESIGN, FLIP TEMPLATE OVER SO AS
TO REVERSE IT AND REPEAT YOUR DESIGN.   THERE WILL BE MORE FEATHERS ON THE
OUTSIDE OF THE DESIGN THAN ON THE INSIDE.

I RELY ON MY OWN EYE AND MY GUIDLINES RATHER THAN THE NOTCHED MARKINGS ON
MOST TEMPLATES. FEATHER DESIGNS ARE FUN TO DO BECAUSE THEY NEED NOT BE PRECISE
TO BE BEAUTIFUL AND ARE SUITED TO "EASING" IN WHERE NEED BE.

THE AMISH FREQUENTLY USED FEATHER DESIGNS. THE LARGE LOOPS OF FEATHER DESIGNS
IN BORDERS AND THE INSIDE OF FEATHER WREATHS PROVIDED ADDITIONAL SPACE FOR
OTHER MOTIFS. ON SOME OCCASIONS THESE INNER SPACES WERE FILLED WITH SMALL
CROSS HATCHING.

FEATHER TEMPLATES ARE USEFUL IN CREATING OTHER LOVELY DESIGNS. I HAVE
ILLUSTRATED SOME OF THEM FOR YOU, BUT AS YOU EXPERIMENT ON PAPER WITH THE
TEMPLATES PROVIDED YOU WILL DISCOVER NEW ONES OF YOUR OWN.

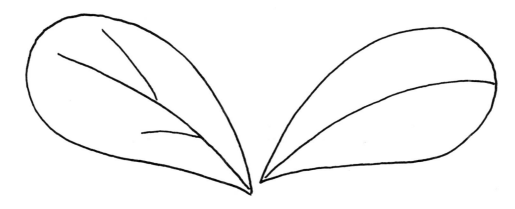

LEAVES MADE FROM FEATHER TEMPLATES.

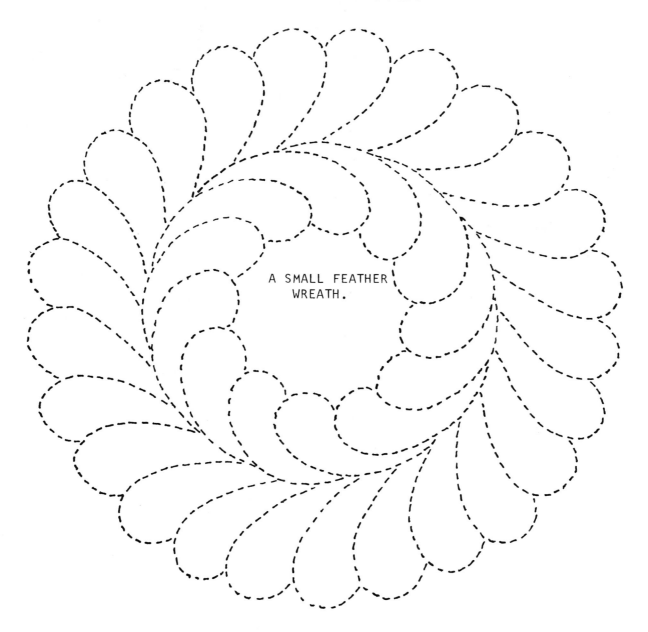

A SMALL FEATHER
WREATH.

HEARTS MADE FROM FEATHER TEMPLATES.
USE THESE HEARTS SEPERATLY OR TOGETHER.

THIS IS A CONTINUOUS QUILTING DESIGN. IT IS GREAT
FOR WIDE BORDERS. FLIP IT OVER TO REVERSE THE
CURVE AND THE TULIP.

DRAFTING AN EIGHT POINTED STAR

START BY DRAWING A SQUARE THE SIZE OF FINISHED BLOCK DESIRED.

DRAW LINES CORNER TO CORNER TO FIND CENTER.

DRAW LINES CENTER TO CENTER ACROSS SQUARE ON EACH SIDE.

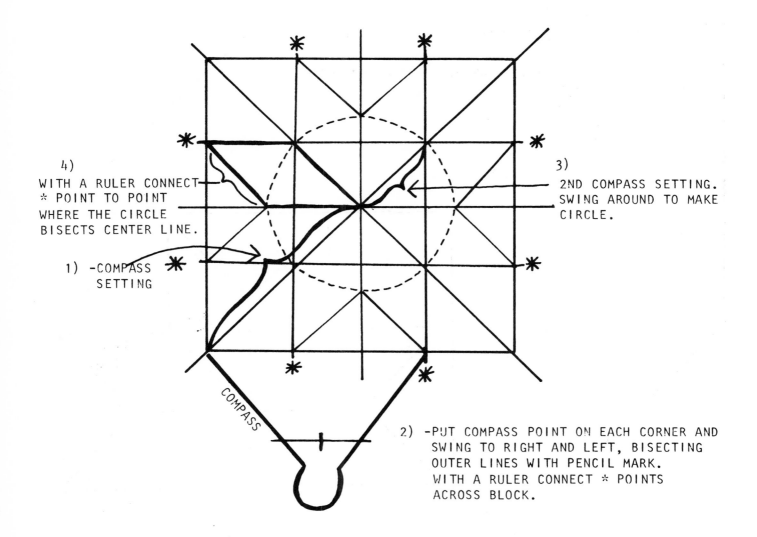

4)
WITH A RULER CONNECT
* POINT TO POINT
WHERE THE CIRCLE
BISECTS CENTER LINE.

1) -COMPASS
SETTING

3)
2ND COMPASS SETTING.
SWING AROUND TO MAKE
CIRCLE.

2) -PUT COMPASS POINT ON EACH CORNER AND
SWING TO RIGHT AND LEFT, BISECTING
OUTER LINES WITH PENCIL MARK.
WITH A RULER CONNECT * POINTS
ACROSS BLOCK.

COMPASS

STAR MOTIFS

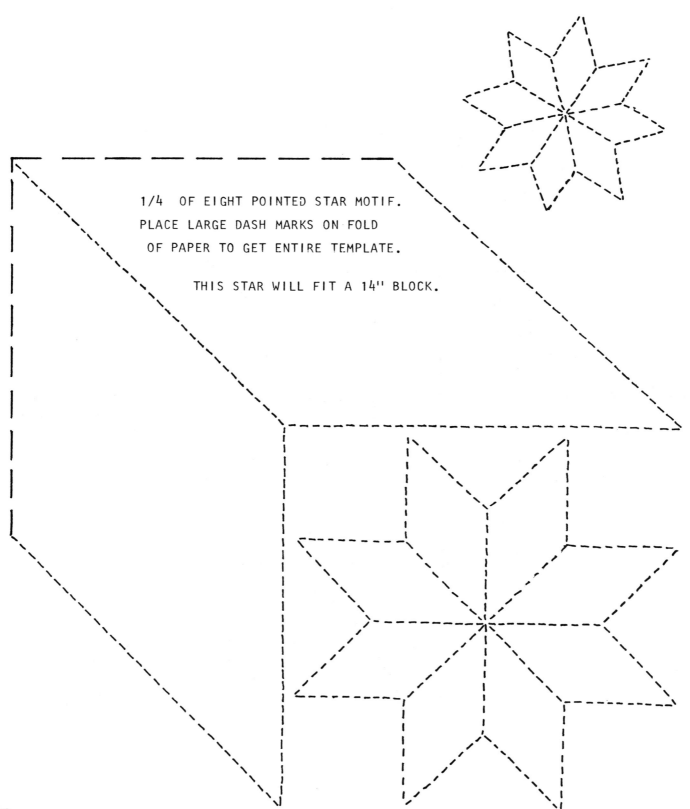

1/4 OF EIGHT POINTED STAR MOTIF.
PLACE LARGE DASH MARKS ON FOLD
OF PAPER TO GET ENTIRE TEMPLATE.

THIS STAR WILL FIT A 14" BLOCK.

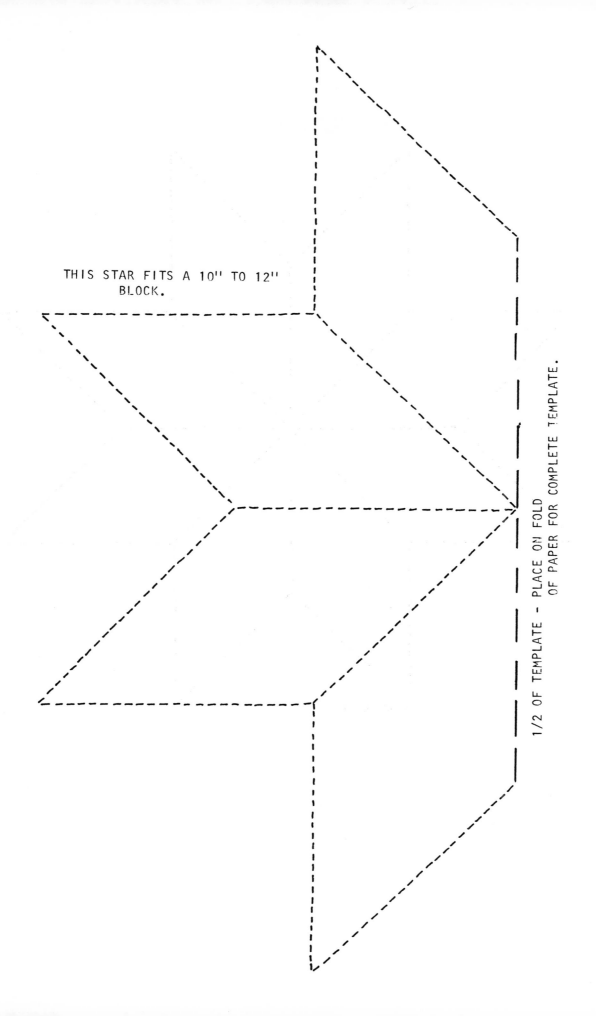

THIS STAR FITS A 10" TO 12" BLOCK.

1/2 OF TEMPLATE - PLACE ON FOLD OF PAPER FOR COMPLETE TEMPLATE.

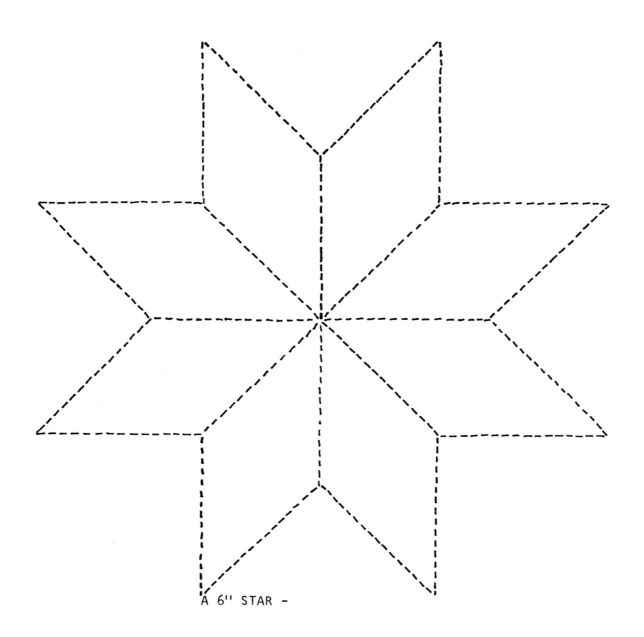

A 6" STAR -

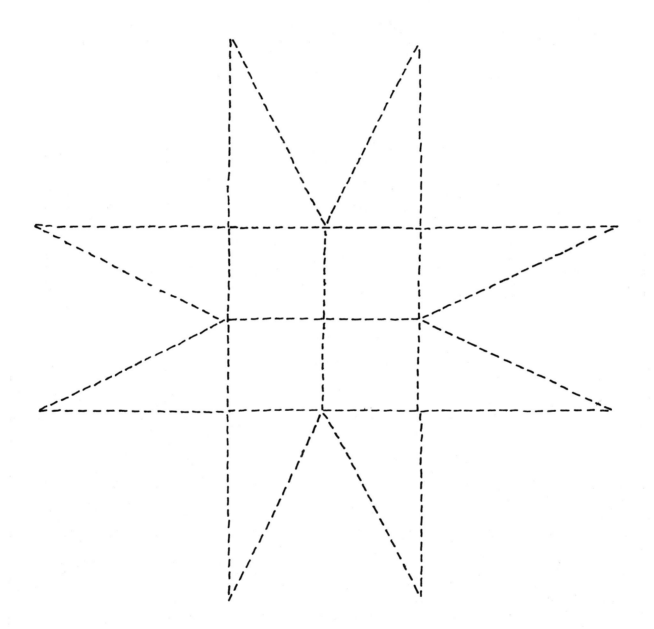

CABLE DESIGNS

THESE ARE CONTINUOUS DESIGNS. CONNECT AT SIDES.

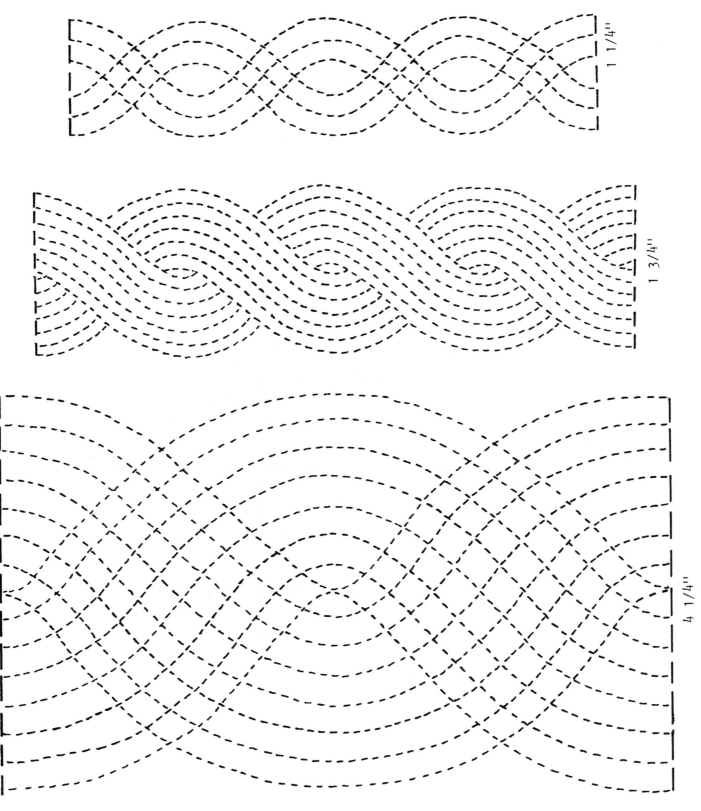

1 1/4"

1 3/4"

4 1/4"

1 1/2"

2 1/2"

WHEN
CONTINUING THIS
CABLE, OVERLAP END DIAMONDS.

BASKET MOTIFS

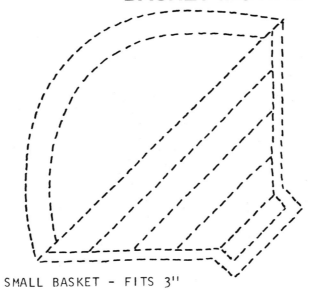

SMALL BASKET - FITS 3"

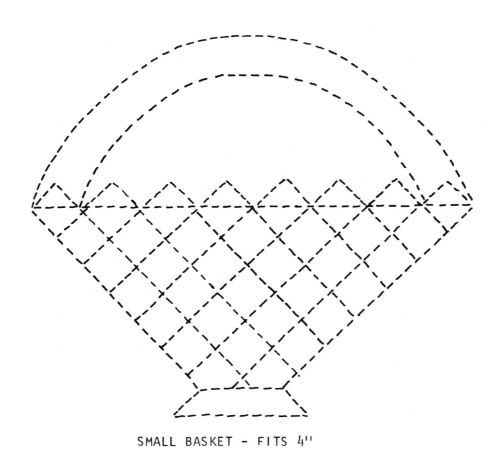

SMALL BASKET - FITS 4"

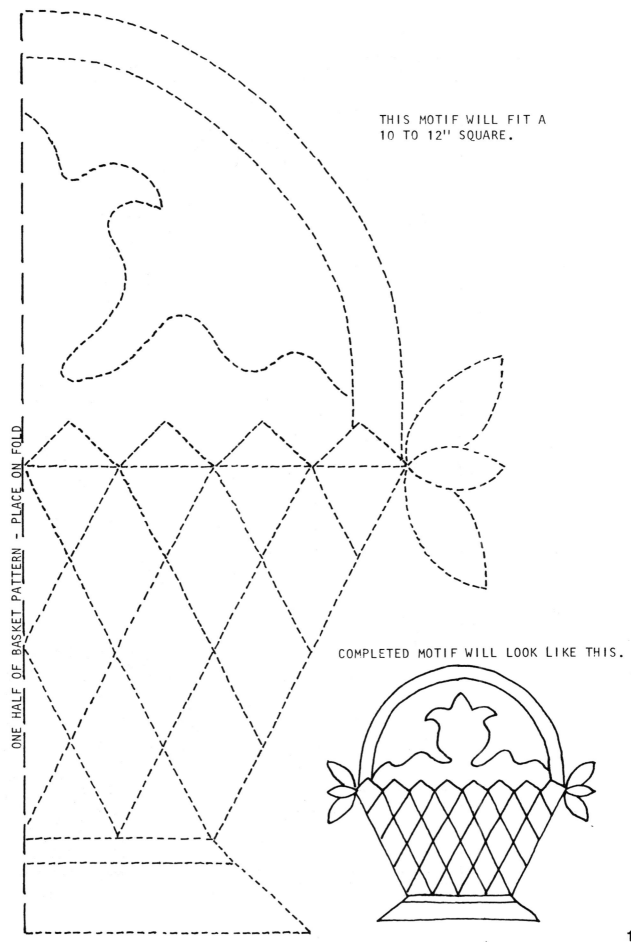

THIS MOTIF WILL FIT A
10 TO 12" SQUARE.

ONE HALF OF BASKET PATTERN - PLACE ON FOLD

COMPLETED MOTIF WILL LOOK LIKE THIS.

119

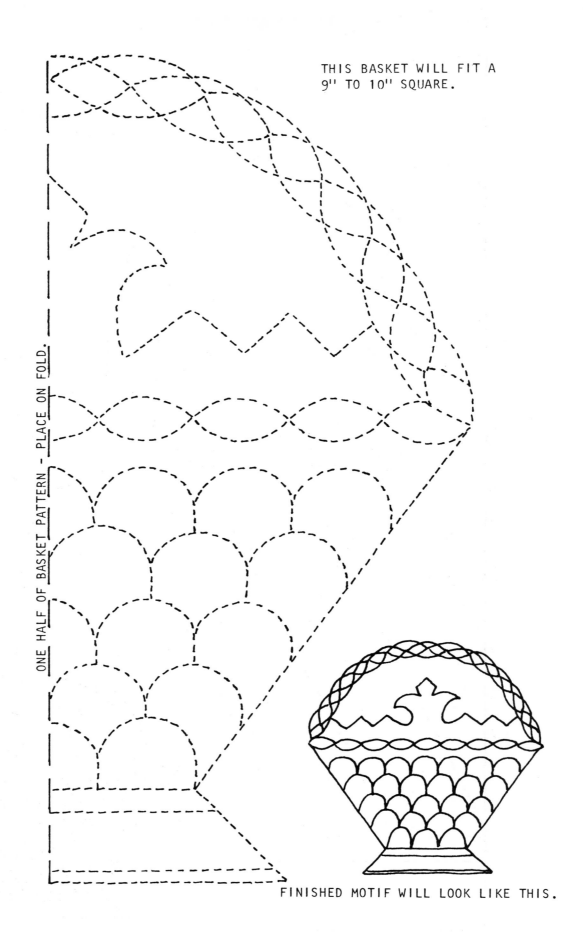

THIS BASKET WILL FIT A
9" TO 10" SQUARE.

ONE HALF OF BASKET PATTERN - PLACE ON FOLD.

FINISHED MOTIF WILL LOOK LIKE THIS.

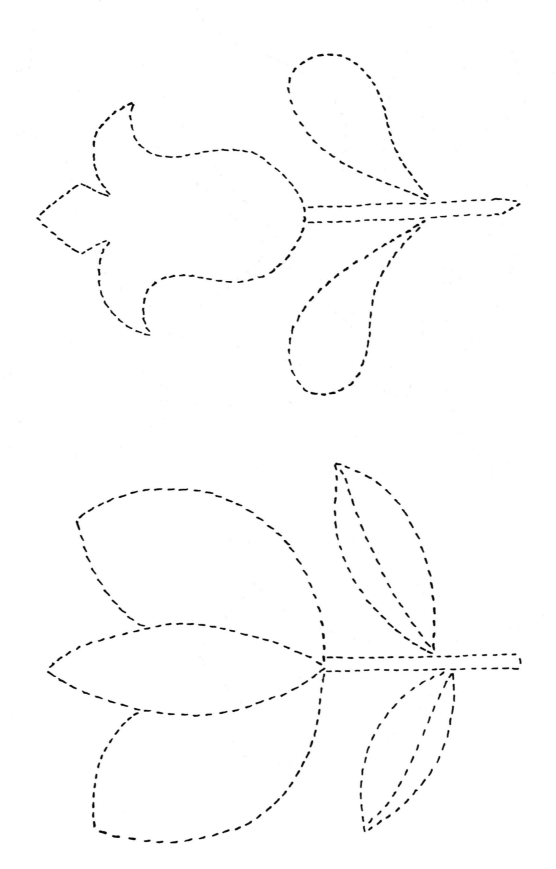

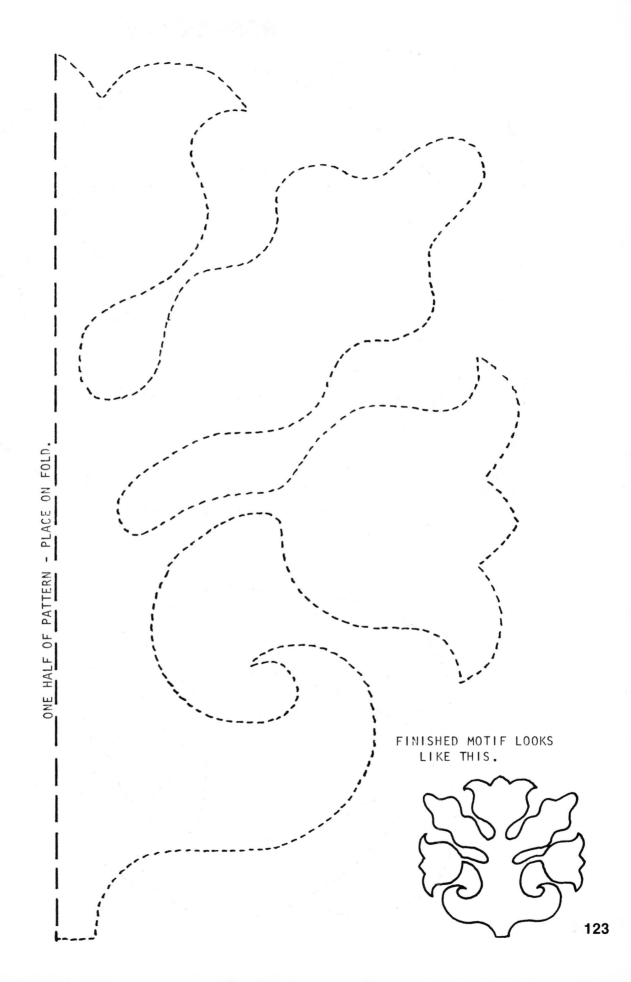

ONE HALF OF PATTERN – PLACE ON FOLD.

FINISHED MOTIF LOOKS
LIKE THIS.

ROSE MOTIFS

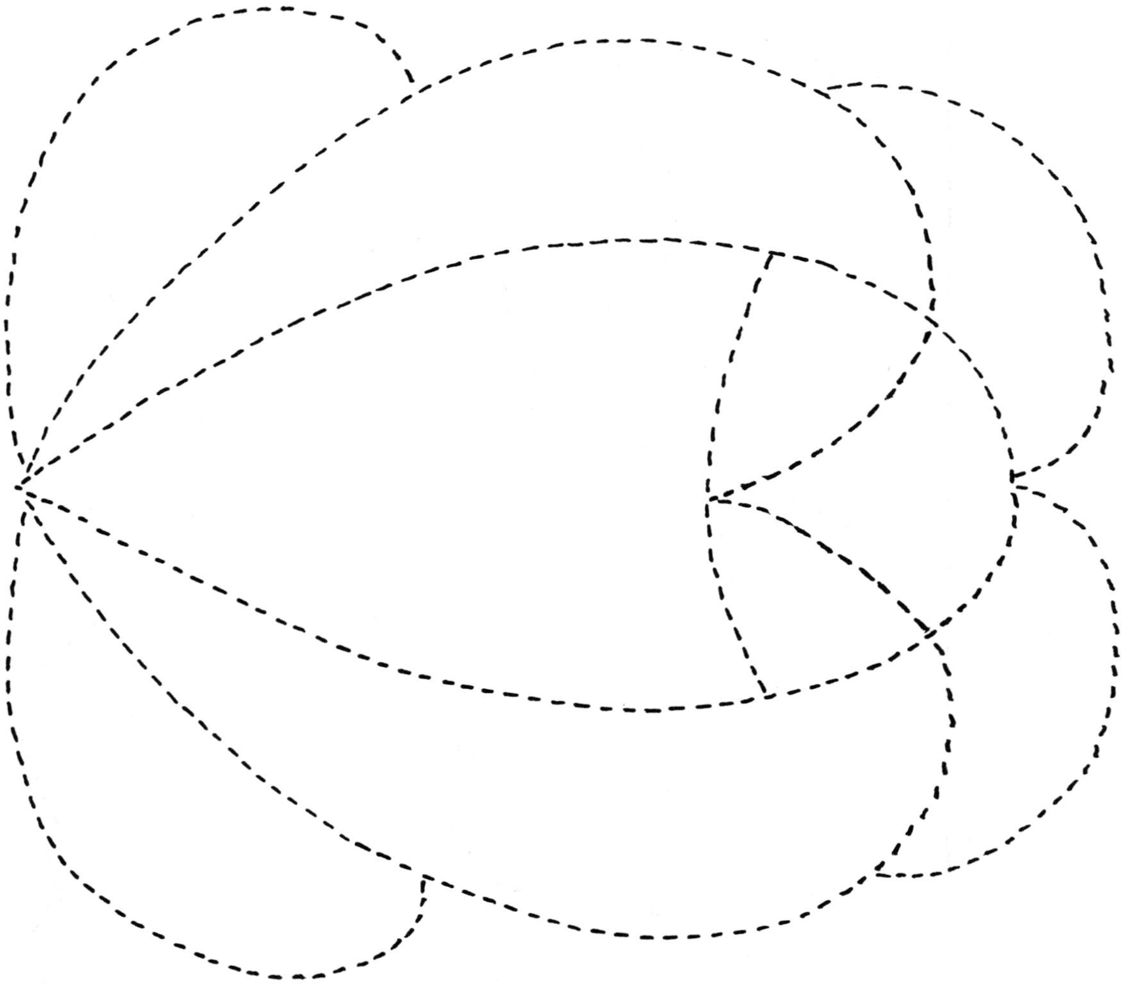

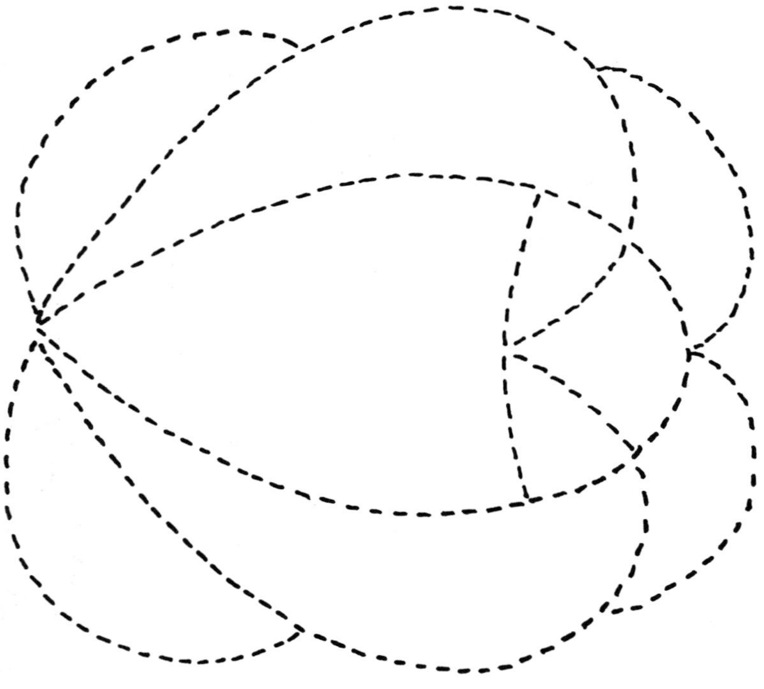

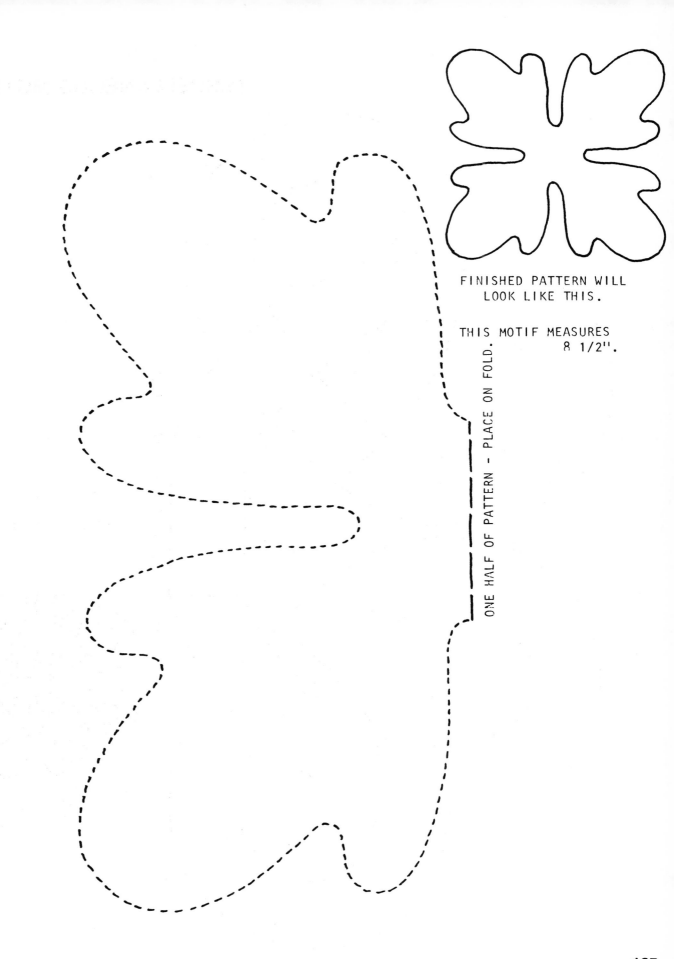

FINISHED PATTERN WILL
LOOK LIKE THIS.

THIS MOTIF MEASURES
8 1/2".

ONE HALF OF PATTERN - PLACE ON FOLD.

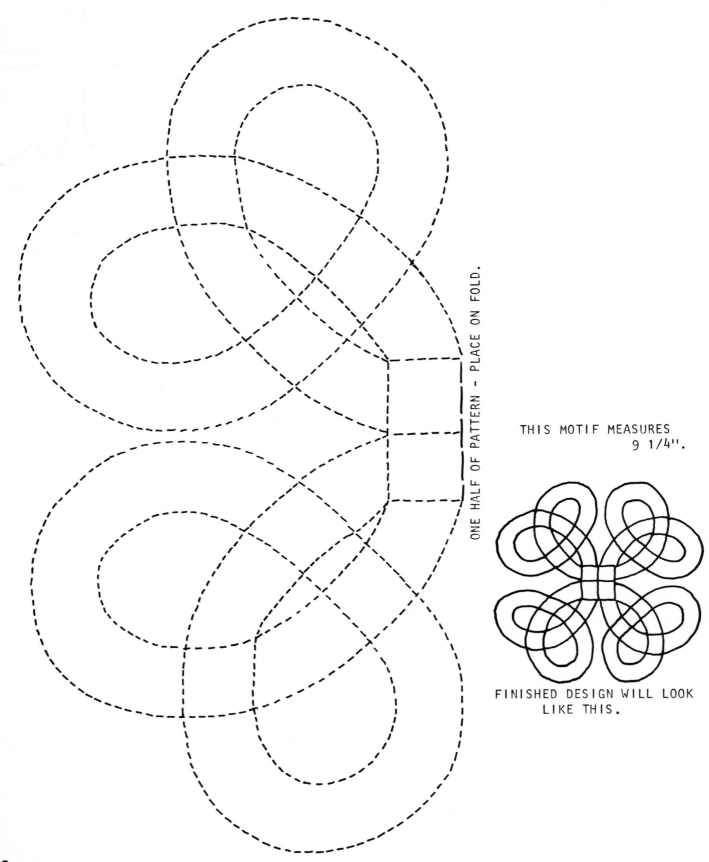

ONE HALF OF PATTERN – PLACE ON FOLD.

THIS MOTIF MEASURES
9 1/4''.

FINISHED DESIGN WILL LOOK
LIKE THIS.

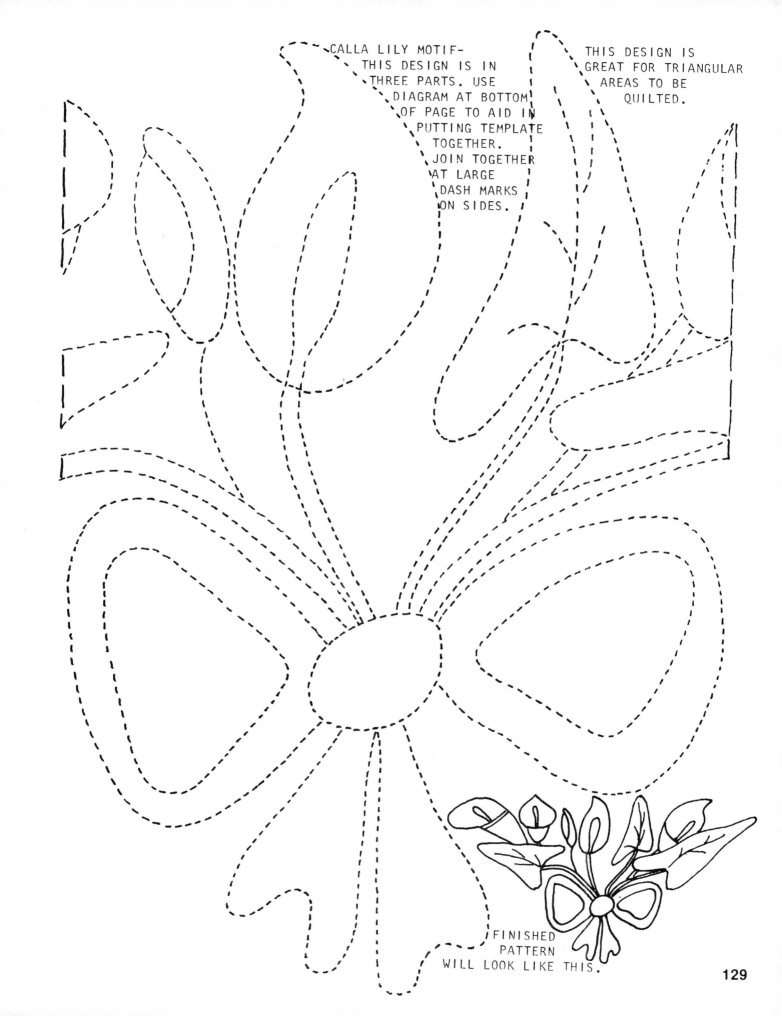

CALLA LILY MOTIF—
THIS DESIGN IS IN
THREE PARTS. USE
DIAGRAM AT BOTTOM
OF PAGE TO AID IN
PUTTING TEMPLATE
TOGETHER.
JOIN TOGETHER
AT LARGE
DASH MARKS
ON SIDES.

THIS DESIGN IS
GREAT FOR TRIANGULAR
AREAS TO BE
QUILTED.

FINISHED
PATTERN
WILL LOOK LIKE THIS.

129

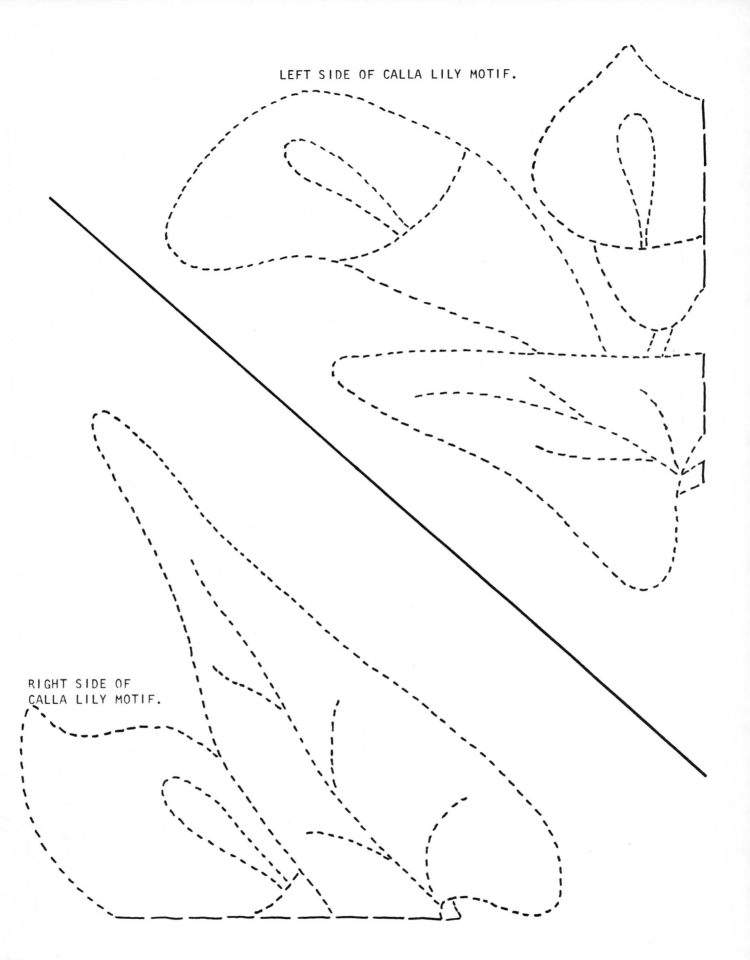

LEFT SIDE OF CALLA LILY MOTIF.

RIGHT SIDE OF
CALLA LILY MOTIF.

THIS MOTIF WILL FIT A
10" BLOCK.

ONE HALF OF PATTERN - PLACE ON FOLD.

FINISHED MOTIF WILL LOOK LIKE THIS.   **131**

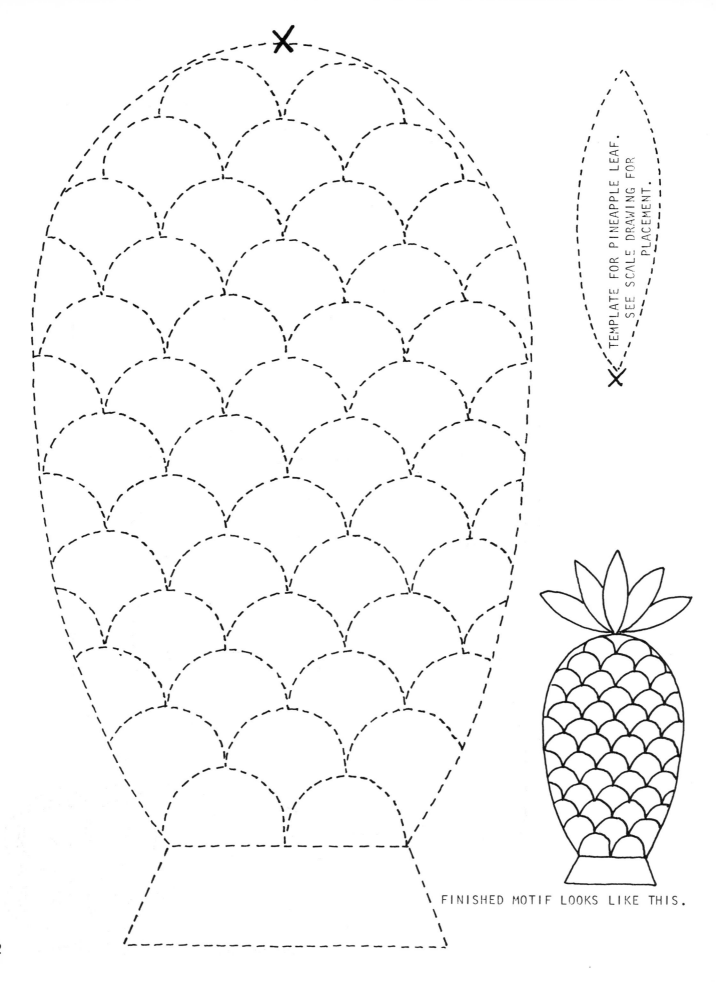

TEMPLATE FOR PINEAPPLE LEAF. SEE SCALE DRAWING FOR PLACEMENT.

FINISHED MOTIF LOOKS LIKE THIS.

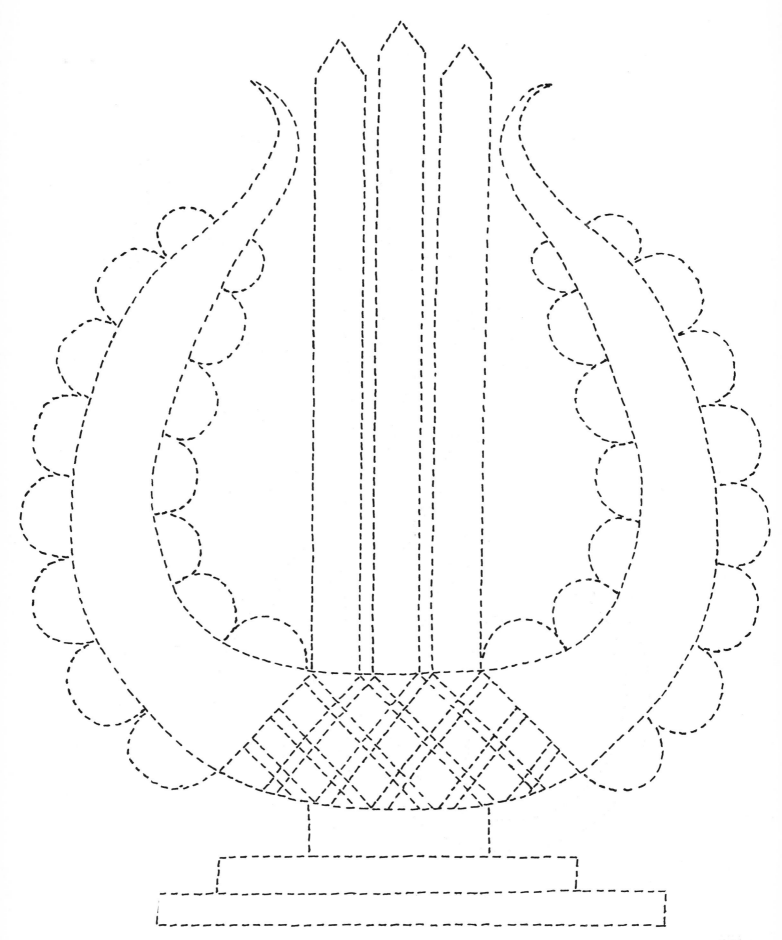

133

CHAPTER FIVE
BACKING AND BINDING

UNLIKE THE QUILT TOP, THE QUILT BACKING SOMETIMES CONSISTED OF PRINTED FABRICS. THE PRINTS WERE USUALLY SMALL FLORALS OR TINY CHECKS. ALTHOUGH YOU WILL NEVER SEE THE OLD ORDER AMISH WEARING PRINTED FABRIC, THIS USE OF PRINTS ON QUILT BACKINGS WAS PROBABLY PERMITTED BECAUSE THE BACKINGS WERE NOT HIGHLY VISIBLE.

I HAVE SEEN AMISH QUILTS BACKED WITH SOLID COLOR FABRICS THAT WERE PIECED. SOMETIMES PIECED RANDOMLY, PROBABLY TO BETTER USE REMNANTS, AND SOMETIMES PIECED AS A PLANNED DESIGN. THESE DESIGNS WERE GENERALLY LARGE IN FORMAT.

SOME OLD AMISH QUILTS DO HAVE ONE COLOR BACKINGS, OFTEN IN A DARK COLOR AND SOMETIMES IN A COLOR THAT DOES NOT APPEAR IN THE QUILT TOP.

I USUALLY BACK MY QUILTS IN BLACK OR BROWN. THEY DO NOT SOIL AS EASILY AND SOME OF MY PRETTIER COLORS ARE MORE COSTLY. I PIECE THE BACKING AS NECESSARY AND ALWAYS MAKE SURE MY BACKING IS ONE OR TWO INCHES LARGER THAN MY QUILT TOP.

AGAIN, I PREFER USING 100% COTTON.

BINDINGS IN MANY AMISH QUILTS WERE AN ESSENTIAL PART OF THE DESIGN. MY EXPERIENCE HAS BEEN THAT, LIKE THE AMISH WOMEN, USING A SEPERATE COLOR FOR THE BINDING FRAMES MY QUILT AND GIVES IT A FINISHED LOOK. IN THE SAME WAY A PICTURE FRAME FINISHES A PICTURE, YOUR BINDING WILL BE THE QUILTS FINISHING TOUCH. TRY USING A COLOR DIFFERENT FROM ANY YOU HAVE USED IN YOUR QUILT. SOMETIMES IT CAN MEAN THE DIFFERENCE BETWEEN "NICE" AND "SPECTACULAR".

AMISH BINDINGS WERE OFTEN VERY WIDE, SOMETIMES AN INCH OR EVEN MORE. I LIKE MY BINDING TO BE SEPERATE FROM THE BACKING. I FEEL THE QUILT WILL LAY BETTER, HAVE A MORE FINISHED LOOK AND, IF THE BINDING WEARS FROM USE, CAN BE REPLACED.

SINCE THE BINDINGS GENERALLY LAY ALONG THE EDGE OF A SOLID BORDER, I LIKE TO CUT THEM ON THE STRAIGHT GRAIN OF THE FABRIC RATHER THAN ON THE BIAS. I PIECE THEM WHERE NECESSARY TO MAKE LONG STRIPS. I USE BIAS BINDING IF IT IS TO BE STITCHED ONTO A BORDER WITH MANY PIECES IN IT. I MITER MY BINDING CORNERS BECAUSE I LIKE THE NICE SHARP CORNERS THAT RESULT.

AMISH WOMEN GENERALLY USED A COARSE WOOL FOR THEIR BATTING. ON OTHER OCCASIONS, PERHAPS FOR UTILITY QUILTS, THE FILLING WOULD BE ANOTHER QUILT WHICH WAS WORN AND NO LONGER SERVICEABLE. THERE ARE COMPANIES THAT STILL SELL WOOLEN BATTING, BUT I PREFER USING A SYNTHETIC BAT. I LOOK FOR ONE WITH A SLIGHT LOFT AND ONE THAT IS GLAZED. THE BATTING WITHOUT A GLAZE WILL PULL APART EASILY AND MAY BUNCH UP WHEN WASHED. BATTINGS WITH A HEAVIER LOFT ARE HARDER TO QUILT AND GIVE THE EFFECT OF COMFORTERS AS OPPOSED TO COVERLETS.

BIBLIOGRAPHY

BISHOP, ROBERT, AND SAFANDA, ELIZABETH. "A GALLERY OF AMISH QUILTS:DESIGN DIVERSITY FROM A PLAIN PEOPLE". NEW YORK, DUTTON PAPERBACKS, 1976.

DUBOIS, JEAN. "THE WOOL QUILT: PATTERNS AND POSSIBILITIES". DURANGO, COLORADO, LA PLAZA PRESS, 1978.

GILBERG, LAURA S., AND BUCHHOLZ, BARBARA B. "NEEDLEPOINT: DESIGNS FROM AMISH QUILTS". CHARLES SCRIBNER'S SONS, NEW YORK, 1977.

HADERS, PHYLISS. "SUNSHINE AND SHADOW: THE AMISH AND THEIR QUILTS". NEW YORK, UNIVERSE BOOKS - THE MAIN STREET PRESS, 1976.

HOLSTEIN, JONATHON. "THE PIECED QUILT: AN AMERICAN DESIGN TRADITION". GREENWICH, CONN., NEW YORK GRAPHIC SOCIETY, 1973.

HOSTETLER, JOHN A., AND HUNTINGTON, GERTRUDE ENDERS. "CHILDREN IN AMISH SOCIETY: SOCIALIZATION AND COMMUNITY EDUCATION". HOLT, RINEHART AND WINSTON, INC. NEW YORK, 1971.

NELSON, CYRIL I. "THE QUILT ENGAGEMENT CALENDAR 1980". E.P. DUTTON, NEW YORK, 1979.

NELSON, CYRIL I. "THE QUILT ENGAGEMENT CALENDAR 1981". E.P. DUTTON, NEW YORK, 1980.

PELLMAN, RACHEL T., AND RANCK, JOANNE. "QUILTS AMONG THE PLAIN PEOPLE". PEOPLE'S PLACE BOOKLET NO. 4, LANCASTER, PA., 1981.

RUTH, JOHN L. "A QUIET AND PEACEABLE LIFE". PEOPLE'S PLACE BOOKLET NO. 1, LANCASTER, PA. GOOD BOOKS, 1979.

THE PENNSYLVANIA FOLKLIFE SOCIETY, INC. "AMISH AND PENNSYLVANIA DUTCH TOURIST GUIDE". KUTZTOWN, PA. 1959.

WARNER, JAMES A., AND DENLINGER, DONALD M. "THE GENTLE PEOPLE: A PORTRAIT OF THE AMISH". MILL BRIDGE MUSEUM, SOUDERSBURG, PA., GROSSMAN PUBLISHERS, INC. 1969, 3rd. PRINTING.

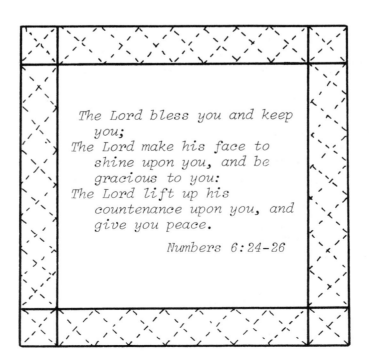

The Lord bless you and keep you;
The Lord make his face to shine upon you, and be gracious to you:
The Lord lift up his countenance upon you, and give you peace.

Numbers 6:24-26